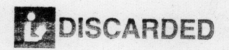

Northcliffe

AT THE WAR

BY

LORD NORTHCLIFFE

PUBLISHED FOR THE JOINT WAR COMMITTEE
OF THE BRITISH RED CROSS SOCIETY, AND
THE ORDER OF ST. JOHN OF JERUSALEM IN
ENGLAND, BY

HODDER AND STOUGHTON
LONDON   NEW YORK   TORONTO
MCMXVI

TO MY MOTHER

FOR THE RED CROSS

THIS assembly of some of my letters, telegrams, cablegrams, and other writings about the war, and kindred matters, has been made at the request of the British Red Cross Society and Order of St. John.

The generosity of the publishers will permit any profit that may arise to pass to the Joint Committee of those Societies.

NORTHCLIFFE.

Any reader of this book who desires to help the gallant sailors and soldiers who have been wounded or have fallen sick in fighting our battles, may rest assured that a ready channel for doing this is to be found by sending a contribution of any amount, great or small, to the Chairman of the Joint Finance Committee of the British Red Cross Society and the Order of St. John, Sir Robert Hudson, 83, Pall Mall, London, S.W.

CONTENTS

OUR SOLDIER BOYS ARRIVE

OUR SOLDIER BOYS ARRIVE

I HAVE not seen any description of the arrival of
our dear soldier boys, many of whom have never
before left England, in the country which is the
destination, for good or for ill, of the majority of
those who leave England on the Great Adventure.
Quite by chance I have on two occasions witnessed
the landing abroad of a great number of them.

At three o'clock one morning, in a certain French
town, I was awakened by the sound of an English
bugle call. Throwing open the window I looked out,
and there, in the glare of tall arc lights, had assembled,
as if by magic, a great company of English soldiers
who had just landed. I could hear the roll being
called. In a few minutes the transport in which
they had come had steamed away, and the thousand
or so young Britons had passed from the harbour
and were on their way to their fate. The great
lamps were extinguished, they were gone, and the
whole thing seemed like a dream. It was a scene
queer and mysterious, and was not witnessed by
any but a few dock workers and myself.

I had forgotten the incident until, the other day at
Boulogne, I saw, by day, the arrival of another transport's load. I determined to watch our boys and
their demeanour on reaching a strange country
that was to be for them so full of romance and

3

adventure. Bright, fresh lads, their English faces looked so red beside those of our darker Allies.

* * * * *

So few hours had elapsed since they had left England that many of them still wore the flowers their sweethearts had given them on leaving. They looked about earnestly and curiously ; their officers, a little nervous I thought, were marshalling them for the roll-call, somewhat anxious as to what the busy townspeople, hurrying to their midday *déjeuner* would think ; the French present took very little notice, for they had witnessed this scene every day for months. Women went among the soldiers selling oranges and cigarettes, and there was a little chaffing between the French girls and the " Tommies," in which the girls did most of the badinage. Soon they passed, as I had seen the others do at night, on their way to a rest camp, whence they will spread all over Northern France, so that eventually one finds them in the most unexpected places.

I have seen them working great barges, running trains and steamboats, digging trenches, building bridges, making roads and railways, erecting huts, and always neat and spruce.

The faces of our soldiers, unlike those of the Germans, are full of individuality. Our boys have their own ways of doing things, and while they are the finest troops in the world for trench fighting, being immovable (and ferocious !) as German prisoners have told me on more than one occasion, they have their own peculiarities in regard to their food and their living.

One of the good qualities that particularly distinguish the British soldier from any other is his insistence upon smartness. Our " Tommy " has his own walk and his own way of wearing his clothes,

TOMMY'S MENU 5

so distinctive that one can distinguish him on the skyline in a country where English, French, and Belgians are working together.

* * * * *

One day last week I had the interesting experience of seeing the depots of part of the English Army, part of the French Army, and part of the Belgian Army. The contrast was interesting. " Tommy " is certainly an epicure, and he is right, for nothing we can give and nothing we can do can be too good for our boys. For his enjoyment we export supplies which, stacked in boxes, form veritable walls of dates, jam, pickled walnuts, chutney, and pepper, not to mention bacon, bully beef, butter, and cheese. The French soldier is a better cook than " Tommy," and he manages with much less meat, but has a great deal more bread, much more soup (which he makes from bread, leeks, and meat), an occasional chicken, when he can get it, coffee, and a little red wine.

The Italian has a most varied diet, as I have described in a later telegram in this collection.

The Belgian soldier insists on immense quantities of potatoes, with soup, cheese, bread and butter, and meat.

Our Army is perfectly fed according to the demands of its own men.

There never has been an army so well cared for. Take the Y.M.C.A. huts alone. They are to be found everywhere in the most unlikely places, and are not, as some people seem to think, centres for the dissemination of cant and tracts, but bright and attractive clubs, where, at the minimum price, soldiers can, if they wish, add to the good things provided by grateful John Bull. Not only are there Y.M.C.A. huts, but there are also those of the Church and Salvation Armies, and private efforts in addition.

As for hospital care, the Royal Army Medical Corps, the British Red Cross Society, the Canadian and Australian Red Cross, and the Order of St. John of Jerusalem, with independent bodies, such as the Society of Friends and the American Ambulance, have produced organizations at whose perfection I stand and marvel.

Much of it has been made possible by public generosity at home, much of it by Government foresight and wisdom, much of it by great self-sacrifice on the part of workers. I have seen him who is said to be the world's greatest surgeon acting as his own dresser in a hospital for privates. I saw the King's own doctor the other day helping in one of the great hospitals at Wimereux. One often hears it said that had the military part of the war been conducted with the vigour and prevision that have prevailed in the Army Service Corps, the R.A.M.C., and the British Red Cross Society ; had the munitions, big howitzers, and machine guns been thought of as quickly as the hospitals and the transport, the Germans would have long ago been driven over the Rhine.

*   *   *   *   *

One sometimes feels that while everything has been done for " Tommy," not enough has been done for the young officers. Their case will require more attention before the war is over. Their pay and allowances are grossly insufficient. Going to and from the front they often have to stop at expensive hotels, and in war time everything, of course, is necessarily high in price. I was delighted to come across something new at Boulogne in the shape of an officers' club founded by Lady Dudley, which is exactly what is required for the happiness and comfort of officers, to whom, after the mud, toil, and danger of the trenches, the place must seem a veritable haven. The idea should be extended to other bases and centres.[1] The officer has no Y.M.C.A. hut, and is often lonely in his comings and goings in a strange land. Lady Dudley's kindly thought and industry in this matter and her provision of much English comfort for the club remind me that a great many of the enthusiastic ladies who volunteered their help at the beginning of the war have found the work harder than they thought, and in some cases much too onerous for health.

Yet there are many British, Canadian, and Australian women doing all sorts of voluntary work behind the front which should, if only as an example, be better known than it is. Does one ever think of the fatigue of nurses, of the terrific strain many of them endure at times when fighting is active? Many of these overworked ladies do not get the rest that is needed. Lady Gifford manages the beautiful home given by Princess Louise in the woods of Hardelot, now yellow with wild daffodils. She tells me that sometimes the sisters cannot get the sound of the guns out of their ears for days, and I can imagine that Hardelot, with its beautiful sands and its golf course, is a paradise after life in a hospital near the fighting line. On a large part of the coast of France from north of Wimereux to Etaples is a long series of palatial hospitals for our soldier boys. I suppose the most northerly on that section is the Australian Hospital, of which the matron and nurses are all from the southern continent. It stands out on the breezy cliffs. Near by is Lady Hadfield's hospital and a vast assemblage of perfectly managed R.A.M.C. hospitals, including even a hospital for the nurses themselves, for they, poor things, often need one.

I have had little talks with some hundreds of our soldiers during the war, and in regard to care

[1] This has been done.

and comfort and nursing, diet and clothes, the provision for reading and smoking, I have never heard a single complaint. The health of all is wonderful. The meeting of Scotsman and Southerner, Londoner and Provincial, Irishman and Englishman is bringing about an interchange of thought that will materially alter British politics as soon as the boys return home. There are the Canadians, too, with their independent thinking and initiative. Now that the Australians and New Zealanders have come there will be a veritable formation, in France, of an indissoluble bond of Empire which, I do not doubt, will have vast influence on the future of the world's history.

THE ARMY BEHIND THE ARMY

B

THE ARMY BEHIND THE ARMY

EFFICIENCY AND YOUTH

SOMEWHERE IN FRANCE

TAKE this powerful pair of field-glasses in your hand. They were captured yesterday in a German dug-out and bear the famous mark of Zeiss, of Jena. Adjust them carefully and look well over to where dark clouds of shells are bursting so rapidly that they form what looks like a dense mass of London fog, with continuous brief and vivid flashes of explosions. That is Pozières. That is how Fricourt looked and how Longueval is looking on the day this is penned. From behind where we sit ensconced in an old German trench there come night and day the bang and the far-travelling scream of British shells. It does not seem possible that anyone can emerge alive from those bombarded villages.

From north to south is an irregular chain of watchful observation balloons. High and glittering in the sunshine are planes, directed as often as not by boys who in happier times would be in the boats or the playing fields. Their heroism during the last few weeks has never been equalled, except in this war.

The battles of the Somme are not, of course, so easily witnessed as those which can be seen from the heights around Verdun, but they are a great deal more visible and understandable than the depressing artillery duels in the plains and swamps of Flanders.

Neither photographs nor maps give much real impression of the great panorama, which is, indeed, only possible for an onlooker to understand when accompanied by one who has witnessed the steady conquest of the German trenches from the beginning of the movement which was made on July 1. What is easy to realize, and so cheering to our soldiers, is that we give the Germans full measure and more in the matter of guns and shells. A couple of hours in any place where the battles can be properly observed is enough for the nerves of the average civilian, for to see battles properly one must be well in reach of the enemy, and so when we have had our fill we make our way along a communication trench to where a small and unobtrusive motor has been hidden.

Presently we come to the roads where one sees one of the triumphs of the war, the transport which brings the ammunition for the guns and the food for the men, a transport which has had to meet all kinds of unexpected difficulties. The last is water, for our troops are approaching a part of France which is as chalky and dry as our South Downs.

Some researches with a view to placing on record the work of the British Red Cross Society and Order of St. John in their relations to the wonderful Army Medical Service in France have brought the writer into touch with almost the most splendid achievement of the war, the building up of the great organization that lies between the Somme and the British Isles.

In common with other writers I have been able to visit the various theatres of war from time to time, and have not hesitated to criticize things that were obviously wrong.

I shall here set down the miraculously changed conditions, from the point of view of efficiency and economy, in which we enter upon the third year of war.

Communication being as urgent as transport, the

Royal Engineers have seen to it that the large area
of Northern and North-West France in which our
Armies are operating has been linked up by a telephonic system unique.   It is no mere collection of
temporary wires strung from tree to tree.   The poles
and wires are in every way as good as those of the
Post Office at home.   The installation might indeed
be thought to be extravagant, but cheap telephoning
is notoriously bad telephoning.   A breakdown of
communications which might be caused by the fierce
wind and electric storms which have happened so
frequently in the war would spell a great inconvenience
or even worse.   An indistinct telephone is useless.
And so, marching with the Army, and linking up a
thousand essential points, is a telephone service that
cannot be bettered.   To-day it would be quite possible for the Commander-in-Chief, if he so desired, to
call up London from beyond Fricourt, for our wires
are already in places where we saw them burying
the blackened corpses of dead Germans, and where
the sound of great guns makes it sometimes necessary
to shout in order to make ourselves heard in a conversation.

Every officer or head of department of importance
in the British zone has a telephone at his hand, so
that he may give and receive orders, not absolutely
secret, by the quickest and most popular means of
communication.   Where necessary, the English telephones are linked up with the trunk lines of the
French Government, for which purposes interpreters
are placed in the exchanges.   The speed of communication is remarkable.   It varies, of course, with the
amount of business, but I have seen a man call up
Paris, London, and the seaport bases in France all
within an hour. Supplementing the telephonic system is a telegraphic link, and there is also the wireless.
The Army Signal Corps is to be congratulated on a
fine achievement.   Over and above these there are

the motor despatch riders, some of whose experiences during the war have been as thrilling as those of our air boys. The noisy nuisance of our peace time roads at home has been a prime factor in the prompt waging of war. Motor-cycles and portable telephones appear in the most out-of-the-way spots. Far beyond Fricourt I met these cyclists making their way in and out and around the shell holes.

A few days later when, visiting one of the workshops at the base, I saw the wrecks of similar machines twisted and smashed out of all recognition by shrapnel, each speaking of an adventure, and perhaps a tragedy. The fact that these derelicts were being examined for possible repair is a portent of the rigid economy with which, on the French side of the Channel at any rate, and perhaps on both, the war is now being conducted.

I am not, of course, permitted to give names of places, or numbers, or the names of the heads of departments, but I shall be allowed to state that the always growing immensity of the Armies, and the workshops behind the Army, is little understood at home, or even by those who have made frequent visits to the war zone.

Mrs. Humphry Ward lately and delightfully lifted the veil a little, but what is required to bring home to the people of the Empire, who are so lavishly outpouring their blood and treasure, and also to the Allies and neutrals, is a continuous demonstration by skilled writers, artists, lecturers, kinematograph operators, and photographers. Now that we have real war news from the able scribes who are allowed to tell us freely and frankly what is happening, readers with imagination are awakening to the truth that we have a whole South African campaign and a complete Crimea every month. But of the war behind the war, the battles behind the battles, employing skilled workers considerably exceeding the number of the total original British Expeditionary Force, we have but faint glimmerings. You can understand the need of this vast establishment if you realize that every part of an instrument of war has to be accompanied to France by its own attendants, its own supplies, and its own transport.

The war plane of 1916 flies upwards and away with the speed and grace of a dragon-fly. She has been made perfect and beautiful for her flight by skilled expert mechanics. When she returns after, let us hope, her conquest, the boys who have escorted her in the air (one of these I met was at school last year) hand her over again to those attendants to see if she has any rent in her gown or other mishap which may be speedily mended. When, therefore, you see an aeroplane you must realize that each machine has its staff. Speed and efficiency being prime essentials of victory, her caretakers must be skilled and *young*. As for her supplies, there must be at hand a great quantity of spare parts ready to be applied instantaneously, and there must be men, in case of need, who can either alter or even make such parts. There must be those who understand her camera and its repair, her wireless and its working, men who have already learnt the mysteries of the newest bombs, rockets, and machine-guns. I take the aeroplane as an instance because of its prominence in the public eye.

What applies to an aeroplane applies in other degrees to every kind of gun, to every form of motor or horse transport, ambulances, field kitchens, filters, and to a thousand articles which at first sight do not necessarily seem to be part of war making.

The Army behind the Army is full of originality It has already improved, on the spot, much machinery which we had thought to have attained perfection. This is a war of machinery as well as of bravery, and among Germany's many blunders was her forgetfulness of the British power of quick improvization and organization in unexpected circumstances, which is a secret of our success in building up the Empire in strange lands.

The Army behind the Army is being squeezed for men for the front. In some places it can legitimately bear more squeezing, and it is getting it. On the other hand, owing to their own burning desire or by the pressure of the authorities men who, in the end, would have killed more Germans by the use of their own particular skill in the workshop have left the anvil, the tools, the lathe, or the foundry for the firing line.

Our L. of C. in France (Lines of Communication) has developed to what must be one of the largest organizations in the world. It represents 6 per cent. of the whole of our forces in France. It has to deal with more spheres of human industry than I should be allowed to mention. Its *personnel*, let me repeat, is being revised continually by medical examinations that eliminate fit men for the trenches. The task is a delicate one. An organization absolutely essential to victory has at length, and after infinite labour, by promotion of the skilled and rejection of the incompetent, been set on its feet. We must make changes with caution.

At various times I have observed personally the great organizations of the Clyde, the Tyne, of Belfast, of Woolwich, Chicago, in and about Paris, at St. Etienne, at the Creusot works, in Hamburg, in Essen, and at Hoechst on the Rhine, and I say without hesitation that, making allowances for war time, our lines of communication organization, superimposed as it is upon the overworked French railways and roads and in a country where there is no native labour to be had, is as near perfection as ever it can be.

And I say more that, difficult as economy and war are to mate, I have on the occasion of this visit and in contrast to the days of 1914 seen nothing wasted. In the early months of the war there was

waste at home and abroad arising from lack of control
of our national habit of spending money with both
hands.   I remember a certain French village I visited
where every tiny mite was filling its mouth with
English bread and jam.   To-day there is enough food
and a greater variety of foods than before, but there
is no waste that is visible even to an inquisitive critic.

Coming to the front, not only in the high commands
and among regimental officers and along the L. of C.,
is a pleasing proportion of Scotch folk who, while
generous in the giving of ambulances, are not accustomed to waste anything in war or at any other time.
To-day, almost before the reek and fume of battle
are over, almost before our own and the enemy dead
are all buried, the Salvage Corps appears on the
bloody and shell-churned scene to collect and pile
unused cartridge and machine-gun belts, unexploded
bombs, old shell cases, damaged rifles, haversacks,
steel helmets, and even old rags, which go to the base,
and are sold at £50 a ton.   It is only old bottles, which
with old newspaper, letters, meat tins, and broken
boxes are a feature of the battlefields, that do not
appear to be worthy of salvage.

Regarding the utilization of waste products there
is as much ingenuity and industry along the Lines of
Communication as would satisfy the directorate of the
most highly over-organized German *fabrik*.   At more
than one place I saw over 1,000 French and Belgian girls
cleansing and repairing clothing that had come back
from the front.   They work and talk and sing with
alacrity, and I witnessed the process of the patching
and reconstructing of what looked like an impossible
waterproof coat, all in the course of a few moments.
Such labour saves the British nation hundreds of
thousands of pounds, and is considered well rewarded
at a wage of half-a-crown a day.

Elsewhere I saw men using the most modern
Northampton machinery for soling and heeling any

pair of old boots that would stand the operation, and such footgear as was useless was not wasted, for by an ingenious contrivance invented on the spot by a young Dublin bootmaker the upper parts of these boots were being converted into bootlaces by the thousand.

In the Army machine shops the waste grease is saved and the oil which escapes from every such establishment is ingeniously trapped and sold to local soapmakers at the equivalent of its present very high value.

Since the early days of chaos and muddle we have conveyed across the seas machine shops and mechanics which must exceed by twice or thrice the total of those in a humming town like Coventry. Such factories have had to be manned, and manned with labour able to meet the sudden emergencies of war. The labour has all had to come from home. Clerks, engineers, fitters, mechanics, quickly settled down to the monotonous regularity of military life and the communal existence of the barracks, huts, and tents in which they live. True it is that every consideration possible has been shown for their happiness, comfort, and amusement. They have their own excellent canteens, reading rooms, and places of entertainment. They are not forgotten by the Y.M.C.A. or by the Salvation Army and Church Army, whose work cannot be too highly spoken of. They are individually looked after by their own heads of departments with solicitude and kindness. The gramophone, the joy of the dug-outs, the hospitals, and the billets, is a never-ending source of entertainment.

The workers are by no means unable to amuse themselves. They are well provided with kinematographs and frequent boxing tournaments. Gardening, too, is one of their hobbies, and from the casualty clearing stations at the front to the workers' huts at the bases are to be counted thousands of English-made gardens. The French, who know as little of us as we do of them, were not a little surprised to find that wherever he sojourns the British workman insists on making himself a garden. At a great veterinary hospital at one of the bases the men living a considerable distance from a town and away from other pastimes have planted for themselves gardens that would be a credit to any prosperous London suburb in peace time.

The energy, enterprise, and spirit of the base commandants and hundreds of other officers along the lines of communications, their tact in their relations with our French friends, and their capacity for overcoming obstacles have response in the enthusiasm of their workers.

Huge bakeries, the gigantic storehouses (one is the largest in the world), factories, and repair shops are filled with workers who are a visible contradiction of the allegations as to the alleged slackness of the British workman. The jealousy that exists in peace times between most Army and civilian establishments does not seem to be known. Great soldiers introduced me with pride to young men who had no idea two years ago that they would enter upon a quasi-military life but have adapted themselves with wonderful facility to entirely changed conditions. Many have brought with them invaluable knowledge gained in the management of great businesses at home and elsewhere.

It is true, of course, that the workmen in our great French factories understand the war better than their brothers at home. They are nearer to the war. They live in the country invaded by the Hun. They see their French fellow-workmen keyed up to the highest pitch in the intense desire to rid fair France of her despoiler. Daily they see reinforcements going to the front and the wounded returning home. There is a war atmosphere even in towns like Havre and Rouen. The war is always present. One day I saw a great number of captured German cannons and other booty of which we hear and see so little at home coming down from the front.

The authorities in England seem to hide our German prisoners. In France they work, and in public, and are content with their lot, as I know by personal enquiry of many of them. Save for the letters " P.G." (prisonnier de guerre) at the back of their coats it would be difficult to realise that comfortable-looking, middle-aged Landsturm Hans, with his long pipe, and young Fritz, with his cigarette, were prisoners at all. If it be true that there be congestion in the docks at home caused by lack of labour, the sooner German prisoners are put to work and help to shorten the war the better.

The war atmosphere and the patriotic keenness of the skilled mechanics and labour battalions in France have enabled the Commander-in-Chief, Sir Douglas Haig, who has personally visited the bases in hurried journeys from the front, to accomplish what in peace time would be the impossible. Transport alone is a miracle. The railways are so encumbered that it is frequent to see trains nearly a kilometre (five-eighths of a mile) in length. As one travels about in search of information mile-long convoys of motor lorries laden with shells or food loom quickly towards one from out of the dense dust, and it is by this combination of rail and road that the almost impossible task has been achieved of keeping pace with the German strategic railways, which were built for the sole purpose of the quick expedition of men and supplies.

There are complaints of delays in unloading and " turning " shipping from England. These are the same complaints that have been mentioned in the Press and Parliament for many long months in regard to the delay in handling shipping in England. In

France it is a question of labour and dock accommodation.   The docks are being enlarged in more ports
than one, **but** yet more labour must be brought
from Britain if greater speed is required.

We at home can help to speed up the machine
if we put our backs into the task as is being done
in France. Our motor-lorry- and other motor-makers
could greatly facilitate the work by standardization
of motor parts. I do not know how many types
of motor vehicles are being used in France, but I
counted more than two score.   Each of these
requires its own spare parts in order that repairs
can be speedily effected, and it must always be borne
in mind that delay in war time is fatal.   There are
in use no fewer than 50,000 different kinds of spare
parts, including nuts, bolts, rivets, and screws.   By
proper co-operation between the various manufacturers
these could be reduced to a minimum.

In order to help economy all spare parts are supplied
when possible from the salvage of machines of the
same type. All this *débris* has to be carefully
collected, repaired and arranged in depôts in such
a manner that missing parts can be found instantly.
The Germans use, comparatively, few types of motor
vehicles and have, therefore, an advantage over us.

As one of the pioneers of automobilization I should
like to offer my tribute to all sections of the motor
transport department in France, and especially to
the economic manner in which waste has been
eliminated.

Scattered among the Army behind the Army
are schools where war is taught by officers who
have studied the art at the front. Here in vast
camps the spectator might easily imagine that he
was at the front itself. Here the pupils fresh from
England are drilled in every form of fighting.

There is something uncanny in the approach of
a company to a communicating trench, in its vanishing

under the earth, and its reappearance some hundreds
of yards away, where clambering "over the top,"
to use the most poignant expression of the war,
the soldier pupils dash forward in a vociferous
bayonet charge. At these great reinforcement camps
are gas mask attacks, where pupils are passed through
underground chambers, filled with real gas, that they
may become familiarized with one of the worst curses
of warfare. The gas itself is a subtle and at first
not a very fearsome enemy, but the victim is apt
to be overcome before he is aware of it.

And at these miniature battlefields, all of them
larger than the field of Waterloo, are demonstration
lecturers who teach bombing, first with toy bombs
that explode harmlessly with a slight puff, and then
with the real Mills bombs which have a noisy and
destructive effect altogether disproportionate to their
size and innocent appearance. The various types
of machine-guns are fired at ingenious targets all
the day long. There are actual dug-outs in which
pupils are interned with entrances closed while gas
is profusely projected around them so that they may
learn how to deal with the new weapon by spraying
it and flapping it away when the entrance is uncovered
at a given signal. Crater fighting is taught with an
actual reproduction of a crater, by a lusty sergeant
who has seen much of the actual thing, and tells
the men what to do with their bombs and with
Germans. Such schools are known to exist throughout Germany, but no Prussian thoroughness can
better these British war-training schools in France.
For those who are not so quick in intelligence as
others there is a revival of the old awkward squad
who are taught slowly and patiently with remarkable
results.

In the centre of one of these schools there arrived,
while I was on the scene, a great number of German
prisoners on their way to the Base. I do not know

how many young soldiers just landed from England
were being trained that day. Certainly many, many
thousands, and I do not wonder that the prisoners
were amazed at the spectacle before them. One of
them frankly confessed in excellent English that his
comrades were under the impression that we had no
men left.

The food supplied to these German prisoners
here, as everywhere, was excellent and they did
not hesitate to say so. Temporary baths and other
washing arrangements were fitted up for them, they
had an abundance of tobacco, and were just as com-
fortably off in their tents as our soldiers not actually
in barracks. Their condition on arrival here, as
elsewhere, was appalling. Imprisoned in their
trenches by our barrage of fire, they had been deprived
of many of the necessities of life for days, and on their
arrival ate ravenously. Most of them were Prussian
Guards and Bavarians, and the number who had the
Iron Cross ribbon in their button-holes was eloquent
testimony to the type of enemy troops our New Armies
have been fighting.

If there be loss of time and energy in the Army
behind the Army it may be found in one or two of the
clerical establishments, which might be carefully
modernized. In some of these departments it is
said that men of military age are still engaged. If
this be so, there is still a certain supply of superfluous
middle-aged clerical labour at home that might be
gradually introduced.

There is beyond question a growing demand for
the filling up of more and more forms in connexion
with the Army. It is a disease which should be
checked now before it becomes a hindrance to efficient
working. In some of the clerical departments the
use of modern files and indexes does not seem to be
general, but this does not apply to all departments.
for I saw many that were quite up-to-date.

In one great branch is kept a complete record of every British soldier, from the hour of his arrival in France to his departure, or death. Think of the countless essential letters, and forms that must necessarily be filled up, to achieve that end efficiently and with accuracy.

Another department, which exists for the satisfaction of relatives, and possible decisions in the Court of Probate, keeps an exact record of the time of death and place of burial of every officer and private soldier in France, whether he comes from the British Islands or the Dominions. Such establishments necessarily demand the use of much clerical labour.

It should be remembered always, in regard to such a department as that which follows the course of every soldier in France, that Tommy is a difficult person to deal with. It is more than possible that there is a considerable number of men who have been reported as missing and dead who are not missing or dead at all. One case was discovered whilst I was at a certain office. It was that of a soldier who had been reported missing for more than a year but who was found in comfortable surroundings doing duty as an Army cook in a totally different part of the field from that in which he disappeared.

There are countless departments of which the public knows nothing. I have only space and time to deal with one more. It is that which watches over the recovery of the effects of dead men and officers. There are separate departments for each, but I only saw that affecting the men.

The work begins on the battlefield and in the hospitals, where I saw the dead bodies being reverently searched. A list is carefully made there and then, and that list accompanies the little familiar belongings which are a part of every man's life to one of the great bases on the lines of communication. The bag is there opened by two clerks, who check it once more, securely fastening it, and sending it home, where it eventually reaches the next-of-kin. I watched the opening of one such pathetic parcel during the final checking. It contained a few pence, a pipe, a photo of wife and bairn, a trench ring made of the aluminium of an enemy fuze, a small diary, and a pouch. It was all the man had.

They told me that nearly every soldier carries a souvenir. In one haversack was found a huge piece of German shell which had probably been carried for months. The relatives at home set great store on these treasures, and though the proper officials to address are those at the War Office, London, the people in France are often in receipt of indignant letters from relatives asking why this or that trifle has not been returned.

One of them which arrived that day said, " I gave my son to the war, you have had him, you might at least return all his property intact. Where are the pair of gloves and zinc ointment he had with him ? "

The work of collecting these last mementos of the dead is carried out with promptness, care, and very kindly feeling, despite the monotony of the task, which begins in the morning and goes on to the evening, a task which is increasing daily with the size of the war.

THE WOMEN ARE SPLENDID

c 2

THE WOMEN ARE SPLENDID [1]

WOMAN's part in the war ; not the tender nursing part—that was expected by all—but the great share she is taking in what was once man's work is one of the great surprises.

There is just a note of wounded vanity in the confessions of thousands of men who have to admit to-day that, unknown to themselves, they have been performing tasks which are now proved to have been women's work. Across the Channel, in France, women have always successfully managed large businesses. There is a large number of cases in point : Mme. Pommery, whose champagne sparkles around the world ; Mme. Duval, who organized the popular restaurants that were the forerunners of so many in London ; Mme. Paquin, who succeeded her husband in the great modiste business ; Mme. Curie, who discovered radium. Women play a prominent part in French politics, French business, French science, French agriculture, and in French affairs generally.

Throughout the English-speaking world we have always prided ourselves on sheltering our woman-kind. We have not, for example, cared to see them working in the fields and at the heavier forms of manual labour. There has been a great deal of self-deception about it, because, after all, women have

---

[1] This article was among the first to call attention to the great part played by women in the effective waging of war.

performed heavy tasks in factories for a century or more. And we must not forget our old friends, the chainmakers of Cradley Heath.

Again, from the days of Florence Nightingale the noble work of nursing our sick and carrying on the service of our hospitals has been to an increasing extent in the hands of women. In no field have they displayed a higher competence, a more sublime devotion ; and few indeed are they who have not at some time or other in their lives incurred a tremendous debt to the British hospital nurse. Again, here and there before the war, gifted women, such as Elizabeth Fry and Octavia Hill, showed the way in social reform among us, and lately women have shone in journalism and in municipal work.

Yet, despite these very striking exceptions, the war has already proved that woman has not hitherto been given her opportunity in most parts of the Empire. For some years her cause was obscured by the hysteria of the Suffragettes. To-day it begins to look as though the votes-for-women demonstrations were but manifestations of the tremendous pent-up energy of more than half the nation.

Women have taken to every kind of war work with a rapidity and adaptability that have certainly not been shown by all the ruling sex. It has been openly admitted that in many munition factories women, in their eagerness to defeat the enemy, are producing a greater output of energy each day than men working in the same shops.

Women have successfully initiated themselves into new kinds of war work which had hitherto been regarded as coming only within man's sphere. Sometimes, however, woman, in the excess of her zeal, is doing work she ought not to be permitted to do in the interest of the race and the nation. Delicately-bred women should not be allowed to push trades-men's heavy tricycles or undertake the duties of

grooms and ostlers. But there are still wide fields
of opportunity for them in most of the indoor and
many of the outdoor occupations.

These vocations will remain open in those dim and
distant days, known as " After the war," when no
self-respecting male will again be seen matching
ribbons behind counters, typewriting, standing behind
aldermanic chairs, or playing the piano at kinema
theatres. The men who have been bomb-throwing
will have no appetite for the hundred-and-one gentle
and essentially feminine pursuits by which they have
hitherto earned their living.

Every woman who is releasing a man from his work
is helping in the war. And—to do them justice—
women, with their characteristic intuition, saw that
fact instantly. Every woman so engaged is showing
the world the real capacity of her sex for many
kinds of labour, and is also helping the country to
progress towards a much-desired goal : the more equal
distribution of money among the people.

Before the war, in dreary, manless suburbs and
provincial towns, thousands of nice girls, whose
families thought it beneath their dignity that they
should work, preferred the boresome existence of
keeping up appearances on small dress allowances
to an active participation in daily life. Since the
war these young women have entered into the battle
of industrial work with joyousness and, though the
absence of the best of the land in the war zone is
unhappily delaying the marriage to which every
patriotic woman looks forward, they have the great
satisfaction of knowing that, whether they be women
doctors, women dentists, women clerks, women
ticket collectors, or engaged in any other profession,
they are helping the great cause of Freedom.

A CIVILIAN'S IMPRESSIONS OF THE WAR

A CIVILIAN'S IMPRESSIONS OF THE WAR

It is a strange sensation, that of being the only man in civilian clothes among hundreds of thousands of soldiers.

At first the attention one receives from eyes always either curious or suspicious is embarrassing, and even after some weeks of the armies one never quite gets used to the situation. It is but natural that soldiers have no use for any but soldiers in war-time. Officers and men may not appear to be anxious, or working with great intensity, but everyone in an army knows that he is part of an intricate machine, and that although his part may be only a small one, it is essential to the whole.

     *   *   *   *   *   *

A civilian, therefore, is an intruder, a mere passenger among an overworked crew. Almost the only civilians who are ever to be found in civilian costume close to the fighting-line are members of Parliament, members of the French Chamber of Deputies, or an occasional irregular correspondent. Regular correspondents, both with the French and British Armies, are in uniform. Even the kinematograph operators with the French Army are in uniform, and wear the steel helmet of the troops—as well they may, for a stray shot from a rifle or a fragment of shrapnel may wander far from its intended path, and now and then the kinematograph operator, if he is to take a great

picture, can only do so by getting close to the enemy.
Armies objected to civilians at the beginning of the
war because they feared them as spies. It is now
thought, however, that spies with the armies have
been practically eradicated; and if there be any
spies at the Front, they are not so foolish as to wear
the ordinary overcoat and cap of civilian life, inviting
as they do a demand for passes and other papers at
every turn.

    *   *   *   *   *

One's first impression of war is chaos and confusion,
and the immensity of it all.

Miles back from the battle-line, it may be a hundred
miles or only twenty, are the bases at which all the
army supplies are first assembled and stored. We
will say that the base is the port of ——, and from
that base are supplied one hundred thousand men,
with their horses, if they have them, their motors,
bicycles, rifles, guns great and small, machine-guns,
bombs, aeroplanes, observation balloons, clothes,
medical stores, beef, bacon, butter, cheese, jam,
pickles, pepper, salt, shells of all sizes, cartridges,
forage, harness, carts, portable hospitals, ambulance-
wagons, games, and a hundred and one other things
which will suggest themselves to any person who has
had something to do with the equipment of a single
soldier since the war began. All these supplies have
to be kept at high-water mark in regular daily rotation,
and one easily understands how it is that in the British
Army the all-round cost of a soldier is between five
and six pounds a week. Realising that what one sees
before one are only the supplies for one hundred
thousand men, it requires very little effort of the
imagination to picture the colossal stores needed
for the four millions of men who are fighting in Belgium and France alone.

The first impression, therefore, of war, is the immensity and complication of it.

The next and more mature impression that one gets is that now war has settled down to a regular business, it proceeds at the bases with the clockwork regularity of a great business.

*   *   *   *   *

Near most of the bases are the base hospitals. On what a gigantic scale are preparations made for the casualties in modern war ! How truly wonderful are these hospitals, whether they be of the Royal Army Medical Corps, the British Red Cross Society, or the Order of St. John of Jerusalem ! If there has been much fighting recently, the hotels which have been turned into hospitals and the remarkable hut hospitals will be filled. There never was a more wonderful work done in the world's history than the care of the wounded soldiers of the British Empire in this great struggle. On the north-west of France, between Etaples and Wimereux, are literally miles of hut hospitals, situated on high, dry ground, on well-built foundations, with well-made roads, electric light, and perfect operating theatres and dental parlours—hospitals just as good as the very best of their kind in our great cities at home, and staffed by men in the highest position in the medical profession, many of them having given up large practices in London, Montreal, or Sydney, as the case may be.[1] Elsewhere behind the lines are other hospitals of various types. To these establishments are attached wonderful convoys of ambulances.

*   *   *   *   *

Though the precision and violence of modern weapons may have greatly increased the danger of warfare, science, Listerism, and mechanical ingenuity have come to the rescue by providing all sorts of means by which the lives of the wounded are saved. Chief among these is the motor-ambulance, which

[1] Elsewhere in this volume I have dealt with the Medical Services in a chapter entitled ": The War Doctors."

swiftly brings the wounded man from the casualty clearing-station in the field to a hospital where he is more thoroughly attended to, and then direct or to railhead for dispatch to the nearest base hospital. It is wonderful to think that there are men who have been seriously wounded, given due medical attention, taken to the base, and brought to London, all in less than eighteen hours.

In addition to land hospitals, there are floating hospitals, most beautifully fitted up, literally sea-palaces for the wounded. John Bull has indeed taken good care of those who have suffered in his cause. Let us hope, *and see to it, that he will be as thoughtful for the disabled and their dependents in the future.*

* * * * * *

Leaving the base, one is naturally anxious to reach actual warfare as speedily as one can. So much has been written about the British and the Belgian trenches, in which I have often stood, that I think it would be more interesting if I described in detail the approach to the great battle of Verdun, one of the greatest struggles in the history of the world.

Verdun is in Eastern France, about one hunded and fifty miles from Paris, and the battle zone begins long, long before you get to the neighbour-hood of Verdun itself. I went to Verdun by auto-car. The railways, of course, are blocked with cannon, ammunition, food, and troops.

Long before reaching the front, twenty-five miles from the battle, it had been obvious that we were approaching some great event. Whole villages were filled with soldiers, resting or waiting to be called into the line. There were great fields full of artillery, " parks," as they are called, and vast plains covered with wagons at close intervals. As for wheeled vehicles, whenever I see one now I think of the war. Soldiers frequently travel by motor-omni-buses of all kinds from their rest places to the threshold of the firing-line, but there are in Europe hundreds of thousands, I might say millions, of horse vehicles of all sizes and shapes. Both England and France have responded wonderfully to the call for transport.

In August, 1914, we at once requisitioned trades-men's delivery vans. It was amusing at that time at the British Front to see motors belonging to well-known English, Scotch, and Irish breweries going on their way to the Front laden with soldiers or shells, and also to see pleasure motor charabancs with the names of Margate, Blackpool, and Scarborough emblazoned thereon. These, however, have mostly been either superseded or painted the dull military grey and khaki which one associates with this grim, grim war.

      *   *   *   *   *

Waiting, and ominous, are vast arrays of ambulances, both horse and motor.

Then one comes across huge reserve stores of ammunition. It has been stated that up to the time at which I write (April, 1916) the Germans have fired fifteen millions of shells during the battles for Verdun.

A million is a very large number. People use the terms thousands, hundreds of thousands, and millions glibly and rather vaguely. Certain it is, however, that the French, when I was with them, had millions of reserve shells. I counted certain sections containing a thousand shells, and could judge roughly how many times the amount of space occupied was represented by quantities of other shells of the same size which I saw. It was in this way easy to arrive at the fact that of great and little shells the French had many millions. Shells for the 75—or the British three-inch—gun take up comparatively little space when standing on end.

But it is not only ammunition and soldiers that

are going along the road to the battle. There are
the great supplies of bread and meat. The French,
covering their Paris motor-omnibuses with perforated
zinc, transformed them into meat wagons. Everything
now goes to the battle on wheels.

       *   *   *   *   *

It is rarely that one hears bands in modern war.
Once, on my way to the battle of Verdun, I came
across something that looked like a war picture—
a squadron of lancers with their pennants gaily
streaming, preceded by a corps of buglers.

For the rest this war is a horrible, grim, mechanical
business.   Bravery, of course, still counts, and British
and French bravery has done much to meet the
superiority in big guns which the Germans undoubtedly had at the beginning.

Considerably away from the firing-line, five, eight,
ten, or even twenty-five miles, are the headquarters
of the various armies. War is not directed from the
battlefield as of yore. The idea of Napoleon and
Wellington eyeing each other through telescopes,
which it is alleged they did, seems ridiculous to a
modern soldier who has not seen the little field of
Waterloo. The German and French generals at
the battle of Verdun were always at least twenty
miles apart. The headquarters of a general might
be the headquarters of a railway contractor, with
its maps, plans, clerks, typewriters, and innumerable
telephones. There is nearly always a wireless station
outside, where the various *communiqués* can be
read.

My experience of such headquarters, and I have
been to a good many, is that there is apparently
less excited discussion of the particular battle than
you may witness at home between any two people
talking of it in the club or railway train. There is
no lack of information, because the staff at headquarters is linked up by long-distance and other telephones

with the soldier in the field. There is generally distributed each day a little bulletin giving the soldier some idea of what is going on. Otherwise, existing as he does in a line that is hundreds of miles in length, he would have the vaguest notion of what is taking place. Indeed, it is the newspaper that has come from London or from Paris which is his chief source of information, for in those great centres all the news of the war is collected, explained by maps, and put forth in a way that makes it extremely easy for the soldier on the spot to understand. I followed the battle of Verdun from a large staff map, but also from maps cut from London newspapers, which I found to be wonderfully accurate.

* * * * *

Once inside the final cordon of sentries, the civilian at the war attracts but very little attention. People do not know who he is and do not care, but they realize that he could not have got there without proper authority, and as everybody is very busy with his own part of the great affair, the civilian sinks into the comparative insignificance which he should rightly occupy. My own personal feeling was one of regret that I was not able to do something to help in what was going on.

When I reached the battle of Verdun I was confused at first as to what was happening; but I had with me two most excellent young officers who explained the position. I was reluctant to use their services, and was relieved to find that while showing me what was taking place, which they did by signs, for the noise was sometimes too great to permit conversation except in yells, they were carrying out part of their appointed work of observation and were busily making notes.

* * * * *

Does the civilian incur danger in war? It is, of course, the object of military authorities to see that

D

he is kept as safe as possible, but in these days of
snipers, stray bullets, shell fragments, and what
not, he must share to some extent, however carefully
guarded, the dangers of the day. I have had a
number of narrow escapes in the war. Everybody
has had. I did not like it. I do not believe that
anyone does. I cannot conceive that anybody likes
to be in a village that is being shelled, or in an open
space that is being shelled, or in a motor-car going
along a road that is being shelled. I have noticed
that the older and more experienced the soldier,
the less he takes chances. There are chances even
in looking through periscopes at a considerable
distance from the enemy.

There are chances in sheltering behind the walls
of shelled towns, for the freaks of shell fragments
are extraordinary, as are the freaks of artillery
bombardment. In some villages one will find the
whole of both sides of a street down, with the exception
of, here and there, a cottage absolutely untouched.
The effect on the earth of one of these terrific bombard-
ments is to furrow it, plough it, and made deep holes
in it, as though some upheaval of Nature had taken
place. Occasionally one will find a whole area bombarded entirely out of recognition—buildings, trees,
and trenches so smashed and destroyed as to give
much the effect of the two scenes of earthquake I
have witnessed in the course of my travels. Very
often, owing to mis-information, the enemy has
bombarded for two or three days points that have
not been occupied at all. It is not true that every
bullet has its billet, and that every shell does material
damage. Men are so clever in concealing the whereabouts of themselves and their guns in the present
kind of warfare that I do not suppose one shell in
a hundred has any bearing upon a military result.
A great many of the people who read these lines
will have seen shells made, and one regrets the waste

of human effort in this horrible, but, unfortunately, necessary business.

*   *   *   *   *

When I first went into the war zones in the early days of the great conflict the soldiers were as strange to the war as civilians are now, but they have learned much. Above all, they have learned never to show themselves. They are infinitely more careful than is a civilian on his first visit. " We never go along such and such a route on a dry day," said an officer, " because the dust raised by the motor reveals our presence. . . . We never go along that road at night because the Germans believe we bring up supplies or reliefs by that route. . . . We long ago ceased wearing that kind of cap, because, when wet, the sun glistens on it and it forms a kind of heliograph."

*   *   *   *   *

Of the many devices to trick and deceive the enemy I will not speak. They have multiplied amazingly during the long, weary months since the beginning of the war. I believe the British Army, with the Canadians and Australians, is pre-eminent in inventing all kinds of surprises. I have elsewhere referred to the fact that German prisoners at Verdun spoke to me of their satisfaction at being away from Ypres, where the ferocious British are ! Our soldiers are individual. They embark on little individual enterprises. The German, though a good soldier when advancing with numbers under strict discipline, is not so clever at these devices. He was never taught them before the war, and his whole training from childhood upwards has been to obey, and to obey in numbers. He has not played individual games. Football, which develops individuality, has only been introduced into Germany in comparatively recent times. His amusements have been gymnastic discipline to the word of command, and swimming and diving displays of like kind, at which the Germans are very wonderful. It is a grave reflection on the deeds of British or French soldiers to say that the Germans are not brave. They *are* brave, but in a way different from our kind of bravery. They do not take war in the British spirit, which they consider to be frivolous and too much akin to sport, or in the French spirit, which is that of the fierceness that comes to men who are defending their native land.

* * * * *

Germans are naturally, so far as the Prussians and Bavarians are concerned, extremely cruel. German non-commissioned officers when taken prisoners with their men treat their private soldiers with a bullying savagery that is astonishing, and officer prisoners decline absolutely to pay any attention to their men, even though they have been wounded. A French officer, who had been taken prisoner by the Germans, told me that though the Germans treated their lightly wounded men with extreme care, because they wished to get them back into the firing-line quickly, the very badly wounded cases were neglected until the last.

Indeed, the wounded man is not the hero in war that we make him at home. He is well looked after, but the chief object of an army is to get fit men where they can do most work, and to get them forward as rapidly as possible. Thus it is that the advance of new men to the battle from places where they are being rested, together with their supplies, takes precedence of everything on the road or railway. The object of both sides is to win, and while, as I say, every care is taken of the wounded, priority is given to the forwarding of fighting men.

* * * * *

France is so well supplied with roads that often as not a certain road is reserved for traffic going to

the battle, and another for that which is returning.
I often wonder what would happen if war were to
take place in England, with our small, narrow lanes
and well-kept but illogically arranged roadways.
There would be beyond question an immense and
dangerous congestion of traffic. The road, say, from
London to Dover, one of the principal highways in
England, is in one part extremely narrow and tortuous.
I presume the authorities have thought out all these
things, but it is a fact, which any foreigner can detect
by looking at our maps, that we are not well provided
with strategic railways or strategic roads. In France
they have also the great advantage of wonderful
canals, not the ditches to which we give that appel-
lation here, but wide waterways carrying barges,
which, turned into hospitals, have been of the greatest
use in the transport of cases requiring great care.
These floating hospitals are quiet, cool, and well
ventilated, and have been of great utility.

*   *   *   *   *

As the war has progressed, and one must always
bear in mind that each month has changed it, there
has been a great development of air fighting. The
first air fight I witnessed was a very vague affair,
in which neither side seemed to do very much, but
every pair of eyes for miles was watching it. To-day
air fights are very common occurrences, and on the
whole are most dramatic and interesting to watch,
but they do not engage anything like the attention
they originally did. The fighting aeroplane, with
its handy machine-gun so arranged that it can assail
the enemy from many angles, is developing every
month. It used to be said that the air was the safest
place in the war. That is no longer true. A great
French general, who knew what he was talking
about, told me that the air fighters were, he thought,
the most courageous men of all. When I looked
at the modern fighting aeroplane, described in the

next chapter, with its 200 h.p. engine, and compared it with the planes of seven or eight years ago in which I made a few flights, I realized that war has developed the aeroplane at a speed that would not have been possible in peace-time. Yet even now human ingenuity has not been able to invent an aeroplane that can hover or keep even relatively still in the air.

* * * * *

Every one of my readers should carefully think over and discuss the future of the British Islands and the British Empire in view of the developments of war in the air. Let it be realized that the practical aeroplane is not yet ten years old, that already our shores are within less than twenty minutes by air from the Continent of Europe. Let it be realized that aeroplanes are very cheap to make and will become cheaper. The vast change that this invention has produced in the position of England does not even now seem to be understood by one person in a hundred.

* * * * *

The war zone is a world apart. After a few days' immersion therein one becomes so completely absorbed in the activities around that the outer world is entirely forgotten. There is practically no night or day in that curious land, and there is sometimes as much activity in the hours of darkness as in the hours of daylight. There are none of the long reliefs from fighting that were experienced so lately as the Napoleonic wars. There is no longer a going into winter quarters. The battle of Verdun was commenced in the freezing month of February. The strain of modern warfare is, therefore, so great that I am of the opinion that as much leave as possible should be given to the men, and more to officers —and especially to officers of the higher command. I know this is not the view of those who think that continued absences make for slack discipline. I have not observed or heard of any actual cases of weakness in discipline due to holiday. I have, however, met at the Front many men I knew in peace-time who are showing sign of war fatigue, and a tired man is of no use in war or any other worldly affair.

Two years ago very few people had any idea of the nature of the coming warfare. Not one modern military writer gave warning of the intensity of the attention with which each army would watch the other at close range and with all kinds of new and unexpected weapons.

WARPLANES

WARPLANES

SOME OF THE TYPES

LIKE the modern machine-gun, and other war developments, the aeroplane began in the United States. The two brothers Wright, of Dayton, Ohio, were the men who revolutionized the business of war. I have often wondered if in the Wrights' early experiments at Kittyhawk, Virginia, they realized to the full the tremendous weapon they were placing in the hands of the modern artilleryman.

I knew Wilbur Wright and saw some of the beginnings of aviation. Orville, the remaining brother, has behaved with great generosity to us in the disposal of the British patents. We have as yet accorded no national recognition to the Wrights.

*   *   *   *   *

There are four purposes in the war to which the invention of those modest inventors has been put, and each purpose is in itself a revolutionary change in warfare. On the whole I should say that the direction of artillery fire is the chief result as yet attained by the use of the Wrights' invention. Artillery work has, of course, produced by far the greatest amount of damage on land since the war began. Without the aeroplane big guns would be of little use except against objects visible to the artilleryman. With the aeroplane, from which signals can be made either by wireless or by day electric heliographs, the artilleryman soon learns his errors, and, owing to the precision of modern weapons, can follow with amazing sureness the advice of the aeroplane observer.

The type of machine used for observing, like all the latest patterns of warplanes, is now armoured with steel in its most vulnerable parts and provided with a machine-gun in case it should be attacked. These observing aeroplanes should be able, as far as is yet possible, to hover in the air in order that the man with the telescope who sits in front or behind the pilot may be able to see as accurately as possible where the shells are falling. But the observing aeroplane has to be sufficiently rapid to escape the fighting plane that will most certainly be sent up after it as speedily as it is discovered.

A second type comprise the fighting planes.

These should be armed as heavily as possible, and it is no secret that the French are putting quite large cannon in aeroplanes. They may be managed by one, two or three men, and in certain types each of the men can be a combatant. In this matter of adaptability of aeroplanes to air fighting the French, who speedily developed the Wrights' invention, took the lead.

Such machines are fitted with searchlights worked from dynamos driven by little windmills in the planes. They are provided with either a small cannon or one or two machine-guns, and the fighting man is further armed with a long-distance revolver. His work is the most dangerous in the war. It is a game for young men only and for the very pick of the human race as regards quickness, audacity, knowledge of engine, coolness, resource, and good shooting. Such a man must be prepared, if necessary, to dive head foremost one or two thousand feet at the enemy. He is the man on whom we rely to kill the Zeppelins.

The early air duels were of slow movement. The battles of to-day resemble the swift flight of the swallow and the swoop of the hawk.

I am indebted to the French authorities for opportunity of close study of their machines and methods.

I have also seen something of the splendid work of our R.F.C. in France.

Air fighting is changing so rapidly that the attempt at simplification of a complex and new arm may be out of date before the book is out of the hands of the binders.

The vital factor of the aeroplane—and this applies to all the four types with which I am dealing —is the engine, its capacity and weight. The heavier the engine the slower the machine's ability to rise and the less gun-weight and ammunition and petrol it can carry.

A third type of aeroplane, which has attracted most attention but has not really been so important as the first and second types I have described, is the bomb-dropper. At the beginning of the war bomb-dropping was very effective, because the flyers, in the absence of efficient anti-aircraft artillery, were able to fly low and aim carefully at ammunition depôts, railroad junctions, Zeppelin sheds, and other fairly large objects. Some of the early flying was done at merely six thousand feet from the ground. Anti-aircraft guns speedily caused the airmen to fly much higher, and to-day, at twelve to fifteen thousand feet, they have little chance of aiming with such degree of precision. They can hit a town, of course, but to damage a particular building in a town is more or less chance work. Flying at this height an aeroplane could perhaps hit Waterloo Station or the Stock Exchange district, but it could not with certainty locate, let us say, a particular building like St. Paul's.

In addition to the height at which the machine

must fly to avoid guns, there has to be a large allowance made for windage, and also recognition of the fact that the aeroplane itself is flying at from forty to fifty miles an hour while it is dropping the bombs. As a rule, the raids of bomb-droppers are now undertaken by twenty to thirty machines, which fly in the form of a wedge, with a leader in front. The bomb-droppers are often protected by fighting planes, though every bomb-dropper carries his own machine-gun for self-defence.

Almost the most interesting utilization of the aeroplane is for photographic scouting. I well remember discussing the uses of the aeroplane with the brothers Wright, when, in reply to the criticism of someone present as to the danger of scouting by aeroplane, they pointed out that, after all, one aeroplane would be able to do more scouting than a whole squadron of cavalry. Events have proved that they were more than right, because the scouting aeroplane carries with it not only human eyes but the eyes of a camera, and in no department of war work has there been greater progress during the last few months than in photography by aeroplane. At the headquarters of each army are large plans of the opposing enemy trenches and also of suspected gun positions. These are corrected at regular intervals, when the weather is suitable, by photographs taken with telescopic lenses, these photographs being speedily developed, printed, enlarged, and used for bringing up to date our knowledge of the enemy line.

To deceive the aeroplane observers each side resorts to all kinds of tricks. There are dummy guns that actually fire, and, of course, there are endless ordinary dummy guns of wood.

A use to which the aeroplane has not yet been effectively put is sea observation. The British Navy has aeroplanes and seaplanes, and excellent ones too—all the navies of the world have aeroplanes—

but these cannot leave, or return, to water in rough weather. Experiments have been tried in the United States, France, and England for starting aeroplanes from ships. There is a fruitful field for the inventor who can perfect this scheme, not on paper but in practice. An aeroplane can fly in almost any weather. A Zeppelin or other airship is at the mercy of the wind. The man who *perfects* a means of releasing an aeroplane from a battleship and providing for its safe return in any weather in which ships can fight will achieve a revolution in sea warfare as important as the aeroplane has created in war on land.

SIR DOUGLAS HAIG

E

SIR DOUGLAS HAIG

Some Impressions

WHEN history relates the story of the great battles of the Somme, it will tell how Sir Douglas Haig and his Staff had their Headquarters in a modest dwelling, part of which was still occupied by the family who owned it.

Thus it is that the voices of children running up and down the corridors mingle with the ceaseless murmur of the guns and the work of the earnest little company of men whose labours are never out of the thoughts of their countrymen throughout the Empire.

The head of this band of brothers, the Commander-in-Chief of an Army ten times larger than that of the great Duke, is Sir Douglas Haig, well known to his troops from the base to the front, though hardly known at all to the masses of his fellow-subjects at home.

In these days of instant communication by telephone, despatch rider, telegraph, or wireless, a greater part of the life of the Commander-in-Chief is spent at his Headquarter offices. In times of stress he rarely moves from them. Outwardly the life of Sir Douglas Haig might seem to be that of some great Scotch laird who chooses to direct his estates himself.

At exactly five and twenty minutes past eight each morning Sir Douglas joins his immediate Staff at the usual informal breakfast of English life. Though

E 2

he has selected his Staff, without fear or favour, from the best elements of the British Armies that have been tried for two years in the field, there is something indefinably Scottish in the atmosphere of his table. The Commander-in-Chief is of an ancient Scottish family born in the kingdom of Fife, so that the spear of our British offensive is tipped with that which is considered to be more adamant than the granite of Aberdeen. Lithe and alert, Sir Douglas is known for his distinguished bearing and good looks. He has blue eyes and an unusual facial angle, delicately-chiselled features, and a chin to be reckoned with. There is a characteristic movement of the hands when explaining things.

Sir Douglas does not waste words. It is not because he is silent or unsympathetic—it is because he uses words as he uses soldiers, sparingly, but always with method. When he is interested in his subject, as in talking of his gratitude to and admiration of the new armies and their officers, or in testifying to the stubborn bravery of the German machine-gunners, it is not difficult to discern from his accent that he is what is known North of the Tweed as a Fifer. A Fifer is one of the many types that have helped to build up the Empire, and is probably the best of all for dealing with the Prussian. First of all in the armoury of the Fifer is patience, then comes oblivion to all external surroundings and pressure, with a supreme concentration on the object to be attained. Fifeshire is the home of the national game of Scotland ; and it is the imperturbability of the Fifer that makes him so difficult to beat in golf, in affairs, and in war. Behind the dourness of the man of the East Coast is the splendid enthusiasm that occasion sometimes demands, though there is no undue depression or elation at an unexpected bunker or an even unusually fortunate round.

While I was with the little family party at Headquarters there came news that was good, and some

that was not so good. Neither affected the Commander-in-Chief's attitude towards the war, nor the
day's work, in the least degree whatever. There are
all sorts of minor criticisms of the Commander-in-
Chief at home, mainly because the majority of the
people know nothing about him. He is probably not
interested in home comments, but is concerned that
the Empire should know of the unprecedented valour
of his officers and men. Consequently the doings of
the Army are put before the world each day with the
frankness that is part of Sir Douglas Haig's own
character. He is opposed to secrecy except where
military necessity occasions it. He dislikes secret
reports on officers. Those who visit him are treated
with great candour, and there is always a suitable
selection of guests at Headquarters to bring variety
to the meal-times of men who are engaged in their
all-absorbing tasks. If they are interested in any
particular part of the organization, medical, transport, artillery, strategy, they are invited to ask
questions and, if possible, to suggest. In many
large houses of business there is a suggestion-box in
which the staff or employees are invited to put forward their ideas in writing. I do not know whether
there is such an institution in the Army, but certainly
all sorts of new ideas are discussed at the table at
General Headquarters. In every case " Can it be
done ? " takes precedence of " It can't be done."

Nor, despite the fact that the Commander-in-Chief
is a Cavalry officer, does he show any obsession with
the arm with which the greater part of his military
life has had to deal. Surrounded by a group of the
best experts our Empire can provide, most of whom
have had 24 months' war experience, he is in conference with them from morning till late at night. During his daily exercise ride he has one or other of his
staff experts with him. The wonderful system of
communication established throughout the length

and breadth of his zone has linked up the whole
military machine so effectively that information can
be gained instantly from most distant and difficult
parts of his line of operations or communications.
In the ante-chambers of the Commander-in-Chief's
small working-room the telephone is rarely silent ;
and a journey into many parts of his Army proved
to me that out of the two years' struggle have emerged
men, and often very young men, able to do the Commander-in-Chief's bidding or to furnish him with
what he desires. Out of the necessary chaos of a
war that was unexpected, save by the Army and a
few prescient students, have emerged Armies in which
Scottish precision and courage, English dash and
tenacity, Irish defiance and devotion, Australian and
Canadian fierce gallantry all play their proper parts.
Sir Douglas Haig is fifty-four years of age. Many of
his staff are greatly his junior. They are a grave
and serious body of men who have inspired confidence
from one end of the line to the other. They are not
dull, there is plenty of familiar badinage at the proper
time. There is deep devotion and loyalty in their
labours.

It is said that most of them have aged a little in
their ceaseless round of work and anxiety, but they
are all at a period of life when responsibility can best
be borne. " War," says Sir Douglas Haig, " is a
young man's game." He made that remark in regard
to General Trenchard's young airmen, of whom all
at the front are so proud. A soldier who had fought
in the first battle of Ypres spoke to me of the Commander-in-Chief as follows :—

It was just when the Germans had broken our
line and little parties of our men were retreating.
At that moment Sir Douglas Haig, then commanding the First Corps, came along the Menin
road with an escort of his own 17th Lancers, all

as beautifully turned out as in peace time. They approached slowly, and the effect upon our retreating men was instantaneous. As Sir Douglas advanced they gathered and followed him. In the event the Worcesters attacked Gheluvelt, which had been taken by the enemy, drove them out, and restored the line. The Commanderin-Chief's presence was, and is, a talisman of strength to his armies.

On the last night of my visit to this little company I was walking with one of his circle in the gardens, watching the flashing of the guns, which looked like summer lightning flickering continuously. We had been talking of many things other than war, though the war was never out of our ears, for the throbbing was perpetual. It was late, for the warm night was a temptation to sauntering and exchange of views. As we passed through the hall on our way upstairs the door of the Commander-in-Chief's room was open. We paused for a moment to watch him bending over the map on which the whole world is gazing today, the map which he is slowly and surely altering for the benefit of civilization and the generations unborn. He was about to begin his nightly vigil.

JOFFRE

JOFFRE

THE CREATOR OF THE FRENCH GENERAL STAFF

FROM the newspaper headlines to the Man, from
the hurrying tide of early morning clerkdom in the
London streets, to the good-byes of the morning
train to the front; from the Red Cross stir of
busy Boulogne, now become our greatest hospital;
past the cheery ranks of the newly-landed Territorial
battalion, singing their way up one of the rare hills of
old Flanders; a rush along the long straight roads of
Picardy through villages packed with waiting Turcos,
Zouaves, Lancers, Artillery men, in French blue
or the new khaki, to the strange calm of the Grand
Quartier-Général of the French Army.

It is considered indiscreet to indicate the General
Headquarters of an army these days, though the
Germans always know their exact location, and we
know theirs. Suffice it to say that the General
Headquarters of the French Army are at a spot and
in a building well known to English people. There
are very few of us who have seen it in its present
astonishing quietude.

The pride and panoply of war have gone, even if
they ever existed. A visit to General Joffre, save for
the presence of one or two orderlies at the gate, is
just an ordinary visit at an ordinary hotel. Père
Joffre, who has the destinies of France in his hands,
received me at the appointed hour to the minute, in

a tiny room with a long narrow table covered with a white felt top, a room probably sixteen feet long by twelve wide, perfectly plain, and most likely one of the servants' offices in the hotel days of the hotel where his Headquarters are situated.

When I re-visited him the other day I found that he had exchanged that very humble apartment for one rather more suitable to the needs of a man who has to receive commissions and deputations as part of his daily routine. It is even yet a simple *milieu* for the head of one of the mightiest forces in the world. I emphasize this fact because there appears to be some sort of curious, all-prevailing belief in the public mind that army headquarters are abodes of luxury.

The Generalissimo arrives at his *bureau* at 6.30 every morning, and at 7 he has a conference with the six leading officials of the General Staff, or Grand État Major, and his two aides, both generals, and three other officers. At this conference all the reports and despatches of the night are gone through and discussed, and orders given for the day. Lunch is served always at 11, and always consists of the same menu of eggs and cutlets, after which, at 12 o'clock, there is another conference. At 1 the General goes out till 4. He either walks or drives, generally in the adjacent woods. At 8.30 there is the third conference, attended by the same people, and at 9 punctually, no matter what happens, the General goes to bed. He remains all the time at his Headquarters, save once a week, when he goes to the front to inspect the troops or to see generals. A very efficient telephone service renders more frequent departure from Headquarters unnecessary.

His methods are well illustrated by his procedure at the Battle of the Marne. All the orders written by himself were already drawn up on August 27 for

the action which began on September 5.   He pondered
them all out, and then pieced the whole battle
together bit by bit, like a delicate piece of mechanism
which, when the time came, ran like clockwork.

His great work in the French Army was the organization of the General Staff when he became Comman-
dant-en-Chef in July, 1911.   To this is due the success
of the French armies against the Germans, for the
staffs were composed of men who had worked together
for three years and are employed now over country
which they know.

Joffre wears a pale blue *vareuse* or tunic, of very
ample proportions, no decorations, save three gold
stars on his arm and on the cuffs, and the red trousers
with the black stripe.

As that great, grey head rose from the writing table
the impression of the man upon me was that of
massiveness.   Uniform caps of whatever nationality
have the effect of making men look more or less alike.
The great head of Joffre, the iron chin, the kind,
rather sad eyes, are quite unlike the photographs and
equally unlike our stupid notion of what we call " the
average Frenchman."   Père Joffre is from Rivesaltes,
in the Pyrénées-Orientales, and he speaks slowly, and
with no more gesture than a Scotsman, in the rich
accent of the Midi.

Joffre has emerged as one of the great personalities
of the war.   Every German prisoner captured knows
the name and fame of " Shoffer."   Frequently in the
little messages that the Germans shoot with bows and
arrows into the French lines is the remark, " Ask
your General Joffre why he is letting you Frenchmen
get killed for the sake of the English."   There is an
idea always floating in the German mind, from the
highest quarters in the Wilhelmstrasse to the trenches
in the Woevre, that Germany will be able to effect a
separate peace with France.   Should there exist in
that deluded nation of 70 millions any single indi-

vidual with a knowledge of French psychology, a
glance at Joffre should be sufficient to teach him
otherwise.

Often in years back, discussing the war that was to
be, we had whispered, " Yes, but will the French
produce a man ? " One basic fact in this matter is
that the French have thrown up not one man but
several.

*   *   *   *   *

" How is he bearing the war ? " people asked me in
Paris.   I can truly say that General Joffre in the heat
of the Battle of Verdun looks strong, well, and cheerful.
On my previous visit I thought he was showing signs
of war fatigue.   To-day, in the midst of the colossal
series of battles that has lasted for months, the head of
the wonderful French war machine has the healthy
look of a country squire in those good old days, two
years ago, when men rode to hounds a couple of days
a week.

CADORNA

CADORNA

Humorous, Adamant and Subtle

A SHORT, lithe, quick-moving man of sixty-six, General Cadorna is the most humorous of all the generals in the Great War. He has a glitter in his grey eyes that reminded me of those of the late Pierpont Morgan. The resemblance applies also to the character of the two men, for Mr. Morgan was ruthless and kind, and adamant, too, when necessary. Those are the characteristics of Italy's great general, liked, feared, and respected by every Italian soldier or civilian with whom I conversed.

The Italian and British armies have reached their perfection along very similar roads, but the difficulties of the Italians were greater than ours. We were unprepared, but united; Italy was unprepared and distracted by faction.

Among those who accomplished what looked like the impossible—a quickly improvised defence of Italy against her time-honoured enemy, Austria—Luigi Cadorna must be given first place. With his must be coupled the name of his King, for the King of Italy is not only nominally but really the head of the Italian Army, and Cadorna is his Chief of Staff. The Italian monarch is so modest and self-effacing that he is comparatively little known to his own people, though well understood by his soldiers, who see him continually.

He and Cadorna share an advantage not given to most of us in Great Britain. They have been close

F

to the enemy so long that they understand the enemy psychology. It surprised the rest of the world that the taking of Gorizia should be followed by an attempt to bomb St. Mark's at Venice. It surprised us that the Germans should essay to offset the defeat of the Marne by the destruction of the cathedral at Reims. These things do not astonish the Italians and the French ; indeed, they expect them.

As one travels about the world and encounters the busiest people in it, they all seem to share the same characteristic. They all so economize their time that they have moments for cigars and discourse. That was so with Mr. Morgan. (And the blackness of those cigars !) That is so with Count Cadorna. He gave me an hour and a half one day, in which he did all the interviewing, and a very merry luncheon on another day at which he kept his table amused all the time.

His quarters are at Udine, at about the usual distance of most headquarters from the firing line, to which the great captain pays visits long before most of us are awake.

He is a general who believes in seeing for himself. He took personal part in the direction of the final battle for Gorizia, climbing the ghastly hill of Podgora with the vigour of an Alpini. He is a close student of war, and he has all the subtlety of the Italian. In the long story of the last two years he is almost the only general who devised a surprise, described elsewhere in this book.

Nearly all the men at the extreme top of the war know something about the whole war. That is not the case with the minor personalities, even in the Higher Command. Many generals, in surveying their own small piece of the front, think the whole war is there, and judge its success or duration by their own little piece of landscape. It is they who, when on leave, tell us cheerfully that the war is nearly over, or gloomily that the Boche line is impenetrable. Their words are whispered far and wide, and are part of the cause of the rumours and counter rumours of the clubs and dinner tables.

Cadorna knows the size of the war as accurately as Joffre or Haig. He knows about things with which the average soldier does not concern himself, such as the effect of German propaganda in the United States and the value of a counter effort over there that could be put forth by the Italians resident in that country. He knows that the Battle of the Somme is part of the Battle of the Carso. He is a statesman, too, as well as a soldier, and like all Italians, happy to be in alliance with us. His *communiqués* are meticulously accurate.

It seems strange to us that a boy should begin to learn soldiering at ten, but that is what Cadorna did, for in 1860 he went to the Military School at Milan, where he was sent by his distinguished father, Count Raffaele Cadorna, who had married Countess Clementina Zoppi—names of note in Italian history.

At fifteen he proceeded to the Military Academy at Turin. At the age of forty-two he had attained the rank of colonel in command of the 10th Bersaglieri. For some years afterwards he was engaged on his famous " Manual of Tactics," which has been reprinted again and again during the war, with very little alteration from the original edition.

Cadorna sets his face against personal or family favouritism. It is in the blood. In 1870 he had become his father's A.D.C., but as soon as there was active work to do, the elder Cadorna was given the command of the troops which entered Rome in the War of Liberation, and he then dispensed with his son's services. Last year the present General Cadorna had his son Raffaele as one of his A.D.C.'s, and following the family example, he sent the boy back to his regiment directly Italy entered the lists.

With His Excellency General Cadorna (to give

him his Italian prefix) is General Porro, and along the whole of the Italian front are generals who have arrived at their position by the ruthless process of elimination necessary to success in war. Some of the earlier generals made mistakes and are gone, as with our army. War is just what it always was, and victory is for those who make the fewest mistakes.

One conviction one had in bidding farewell to that determined-looking Italian, Luigi Cadorna, was that though genial and full of amusing anecdote, he will not suffer fools gladly. His telegrams of praise and reprimand, some of which I saw on my visits to the various fronts, were models of terseness, written frankly, almost brutally indeed—as a soldier should.

UNDER THE SIX STARS

UNDER THE SIX STARS

A Visit to General Birdwood [1]

Somewhere in France

THE high hopes of the Australasian peoples are centred round a bare room in one of the numberless French châteaux where, nowadays, the air vibrates with the throbbing of the guns. In that small room, the furniture principally consisting of the simplest possible bed, a telephone, and a map marked with the latest moves on the battle line, is General Birdwood, the idol of the Anzacs.

An officer from Victoria received me at the gate of the château, where stood on guard two Australian giants having before them a fluttering flag of the Six Stars. It was a muggy morning, reminding the officer of October in his own country in the late shearing time. We passed through one of the halls of the château where numbers of the clerical staff were busy at typewriting and telephones, and then upstairs to the General's room.

General Birdwood stands 5ft. 9in., has not an ounce of spare fat on him, and is a man in hard training. He has a strong but gentle voice, firm mouth with a slight moustache, deep-set pale blue eyes, and a cropped head. He looks a fighter every inch of him. He is fifty years of age, and has been engaged directly or indirectly in the business of war during most of his adult life. He eats and drinks

[1] The following cable despatch was written by request for the *Sydney Sun* and other leading Australasian journals.

79

little, is up and away at daylight in winter and before six in summer. He pushes his Headquarters as near the front as possible, knows many of his "boys," as he calls them, who fought with him in the Gallipoli Peninsula, by their Christian names, and they believe in him as implicitly as he believes in them.

Birdwood, erect in pale khaki coat with some four rows of well-earned ribbons, cord riding-breeches and riding-boots, is not a man to lose a moment of time. He was just off to meet the boys back for rest from Pozières. They were camping in some woods to which we drove in his open car, which flies the Australian flag. Some of them had already arrived. The sun, which had been absent for some days, came out at this moment, and never do I remember seeing a more delightful sylvan scene than that presented by these battle-worn but merry soldiers with their booty of German helmets and caps, German drums, and German field-glasses, riding and walking up to their huts and tents. Some had already arrived and were boiling their tea, making dampers, cooking beef in the cookers they extemporized from kerosene tins, and eating keenly and heartily after their long, long vigil in the heavily-shelled trenches.

As the General stepped out of his car he was instantly recognized by his men, most of them from New South Wales, who had been engaged in what was probably their hardest fight since Gallipoli. They had dug themselves in deeply the other side of Pozières, and had not left their trenches for days. "My boys are good diggers," remarked the General. "They dig deep and quickly, and their trenches are so clean that you could eat off them at dinner time." He addressed his soldiers simply and truly, and drew, first from one and then from another, stories of the fierce fighting they had just experienced. Some were so tired that we had passed them asleep just as they had arrived, others were full of life and gaiety, and as Captain MacKenzie, of the Salvation Army, known throughout the peninsula and in France as " Mac," said, many were already anxious to get back to the firing line and show the Germans that if they were looking for more trouble they could get it.

I regarded with interest these already hardened warriors for whom death, wounds, and the German guns held no fear. A good deal has been said of Australian discipline. English Australians who were among them told me that when it comes to fighting, their discipline is as rigid as the most adamant commander could wish. They obey their officers implicitly from the moment serious business begins, and their relations with the Imperial officers are perfect. The fact that the young English schoolboys and slightly older lads who man the aeroplanes have driven the spying German aeroplanes from the sky greatly rejoices them.

Their long experiences in the trenches in Gallipoli have made them the excellent trench fighters that they are.

I accompanied Birdwood and his Staff from one portion to another of the scattered forest scene. In some of the huts all the men were asleep, and Birdwood would on no account allow them to be disturbed, but in others they were merry with mouthorgans, flutes, and a captured drum. The General peered in, but would not allow them to desist. Here and there they temporarily formed into line and saluted him as he approached. He had a simple speech for every group, always to the same effect. " You have suffered, but you have done splendidly. Are you ready for more when the time comes ? " and there always came a great shout of " Yes." Many were the stories told. One of how a mere lad, for some of them are extremely young, chased a huge German out into the open, and finally settled the terrified Hun after a hand-to-hand bomb duel. Another of how a Hun machine-gunner fired at the Anzacs until he had used the whole of his cartridge belt, when the German threw his arms round the nearest Australian and called out, " Pardon, Kamerad."

All the time we were talking the " crumping " and booming of great guns was a reminder of our proximity to the terrific struggle waging at the moment. The men came into the wood in a constant stream. Having seen their General they at once went to wash and eat or sleep. Birdwood had always one piece of parting advice to the boys. " Write home. Let your mothers know where you are, what you are doing, and how you are, for if you don't write to her she will write to me. I get dozens of letters by every mail asking for one or other of you."

Once, while we were in the forest, attention was riveted on an air fight of which we could see nothing by reason of the leaves. The sharp rattle of the machine-guns high in the sky told of a prolonged fight whose end we afterwards were informed was not satisfactory to the Germans. It must have been a rare spectacle, for a Hun is not often seen to cross our lines these days.

I left this forest scene with regret, but there was much to do that day. Something was in preparation. General Birdwood had work to attend to. He took me with him in his car, and we passed more and more of the Anzacs on their way in from the battle. Some were asleep on the top of the highly packed general service transport wagons. Those in German helmets were singing, all smiled affectionately as they saw their General, and saluted by a quick eyes right or the raising of the hand to the hat. Mounted men dropped their right hand sharply to the side.

It was a long and interesting cavalcade on its way
home from the battle. The dust, as one of them
remarked, made him fairly homesick. All were in
good spirits, and in spite of heavy losses they had
done well, and their General had come to meet and
to greet them.

Passing through one ruined town and village
after another we came to a divisional headquarters
where, in a small house, some new movement to which
the General had to attend was being arranged for,
and he entered a two-storey ruined building, a mass
of telephone wires pouring in at the windows from
every corner, and inside the busy click of typewriters
and the voices of men working in the heat in their
shirt sleeves. Hard by a great shell fell wounding
several men and cruelly mutilating a young English
officer, whom, in the evening, I saw being wheeled
out of the operating theatre at a neighbouring
hospital.

General Birdwood is one of those soldiers who
thinks it his duty to be in the firing line wherever
possible, but his officers don't agree with him. Two
years of acquaintanceship have endeared him so
to them that they feel they would be lost without
him. He has often been far too close to Death
for their happiness, and they urged him not to
go any farther, but to take me to the nearest field
ambulance, which was No. 2 Australian. Cheerily,
a slightly wounded Australian at the gate, in reply
to a question from Birdwood as to how the hospital
was getting on, replied, " Oh, we are filling up nicely,
General." The ambulances arrived at the gate,
and stretchers were carried in in less time than it
takes to write it. The men were classified, fed, and
those who were fit had anti-tetanus serum injected.
The serum was administered with great care and
speed, and the letter " T " was marked on each
forehead in indelible pencil. Arrangements were

being made to convey such as were well enough to
the Casualty Clearing Station, whence they will go
to one of the beautiful base hospitals, probably
looking over the Atlantic, that are the pride of the
Empire.

We went thence to the 1st Australian Field
Ambulance. Sir Anthony Bowlby, the distinguished surgeon, was just making his inspection,
and I passed the time talking with the wounded
lads. Some were sleeping, others in pain, but in
general they were ready for a joke, and a talk, and
a cigarette. " How do you like France ? " I asked
a young Victorian. " I like it fine," he replied.
" They can teach us something in farming," and
another one said, " Not an inch of land wasted. They
work on the land rain or shine." " Girls are all
right, too," put in a young giant from Bathurst.
" Yes, I should like to take a couple of them back,"
chipped in a wounded Adelaider. I was duly shocked,
but the compliment to France was sincere.

All expressed admiration for the French, just
as the French love the British for their kindness
to the French children. Gallipoli, which all of
them, Birdwood included, pronounce " Gallipli,"
afforded no rest. Here when they are not actually
fighting they have delightful resting camps with
well-fitted canteens.

I asked the General where these men were drawn
from. They are of all types—clerks, blacksmiths,
men from stations and farms. Many of the officers
are of the same class. They understand and obey
each other implicitly. They have exactly the same
rations as the British soldiers, and draw only a portion
of their handsome pay. " We have had no lunch,"
said one of the Staff officers at this point. " Birdwood
eats nothing, and expects us to do likewise."

We drove away from the wounded lads along
the encumbered roads, past miles and miles of

wagons with the emblem of the Australian rising sun and the New Zealand fern, and back to the château. I learnt during the ride something new from General Birdwood of Australasia's generosity to its Forces, of the promptness of the Australian Government in responding to his request, of the great help of the Australian Red Cross. These fine soldiers are making Australian history. They are building up the traditions of Australia's future armies. There is hardly one of them who has not patriotism burnt into his soul and burnt into his body. Many Australian soldiers have tattooed on their arms the Australian, French, and British flags with the words " 1915 Gallipoli " underneath.

After a long drive through the dust I shared a simple meal, at which tea (the national drink of " Down Under ") duly predominated, with the alert and agile Chief and his Staff, and as I drove away many miles along the lines, I could not but marvel at the turn in world conditions that had brought these young giants from the farthest corner of the earth to shed their blood on behalf of the Powers so gallantly fighting for the greatest cause in the world, the cause of freedom as opposed to tyranny.

THE WAR DOCTORS

THE WAR DOCTORS

Their Work under Fire

AMONG the first forces mobilized by the Germans at the end of July, 1914, were the kinematographers and the artists. The German Empire has therefore a complete pictorial record of the war from its earliest days. We have lately begun to use the kinematograph. But we have not yet begun to enshrine by colour and canvas the lives of our men, and when we do send out a dozen of our best painters the War Doctor must be among the first to be made known and perpetuated.

We are so accustomed to consider doctors as part of our daily lives, or as workers in speckless and palatial hospitals, that we have hardly yet visualized the man who shares the hell of the front trench with the fighters, armed only with two panniers of urgent drugs, instruments, and field dressings, his acetylene lamp and electric torch. Most of us think of his war work as being accomplished at one of the great healing places at the base.

If there be degrees of chivalry, the highest award should be accorded to the medical profession, which at once forsook its lucrative practices in London, or Melbourne, or Montreal, in a great rally of self-sacrifice. The figures of the casualties among them bring home to those who have only the big hospital idea of the war doctor, sad facts that should lead to due understanding of this not sufficiently

G

known but veritable body of Knights in the Great Crusade. For the last three months[1] in the Royal Army Medical Corps *alone,* I account them according to the figures published in *The Times* from day to day :—

Officers Killed	..	..	..	53
„ Wounded	..	..	..	208
„ Missing	..	..	..	4
N.C.O.'s and Men (R.A.M.C. only) :				
Killed	..	..	..	260
Wounded	..	..	..	1,212
Missing	..	..	..	3

I propose to set down the order in which our medical service arranges its chain of responsibility, premising my account by the statement that the medical army of to-day exceeds numerically the whole British military forces overseas before the outbreak of war.

It is a little difficult and complex to explain. I find that there is some confusion in the public mind as to the regimental work, that of the Royal Army Medical Corps, and their handmaidens the British Red Cross Society and Order of St. John. But there is no confusion or overlapping in the zone of hostilities.

In the preparations for the great Battle of the Somme, Sir Douglas Haig, thorough in this as in every other detail, himself co-operated with the medical services in arranging his regimental aid posts, his casualty clearing stations, and the rest of them as systematically as his batteries, his ammunition "dumps," and his reserves.

First in the order of danger is the Regimental Aid Post, where the regimental doctor, with his stretcher-bearers, awaits, alongside the men who are to clamber "over the top," the bloody fruits of battle. In the early days of the war, before

[1] I wrote this in September, 1916.

we had discovered the secret, or had the means, to blast our road into Germany by ceaseless shells, the Regimental Aid Post was, as a rule, in some deserted farmhouse as near to the front trench as possible. To-day, as we advance, our guns leave nothing standing, so that what was once perhaps a château is now only a stretch of rubble. There is therefore but little available cover for the doctors or the others before " consolidation."

The intensity of the French and German artillery at Verdun in March seemed to me then the limit of human capacity to produce noise and destruction. But the Somme bombardment actually furrows or flattens all before it. Verdun itself could not exist a week if exposed to the present French and British cannonade. Its volume of sound is so great that at times the very earth shakes beneath one's feet.

The doctor has to-day probably only the shelter of one of our own trenches or any little part that may remain of a captured German trench. There is no other covering for him and his brave stretcher-bearers, who are at once his nurses and his orderlies. Happily not so many of these are fired upon by the enemy as heretofore ; for, as the Prussians have realized that our artillery is the most deadly thing in the history of war, they have become a good deal more reasonable and human. Now that their own wounded greatly outnumber ours on almost every occasion, their doctors and stretcher-bearers often advance with a sheet or towel held high on a rifle as a flag of truce in order that they may collect their wounded and we ours. In the early days of the war similar suggestions on our part were haughtily and contemptuously refused. And so the advanced medical forces on both sides are at last sparing the wounded a good deal of the drawn-out horrors of " No Man's Land."

The fine young men with the English, Scotch, Irish, Canadian, and Australian accents who stand unarmed in these Regimental Aid Posts work with an intensity and celerity which eclipse even that of the surgeons in London's operating theatres.

The stretcher-bearers stagger in with their load. There is a lightning diagnosis, an antiseptic application, bandaging, a hastily-written label tied to the man's breast, and the wounded one is borne off and away in the open to the next stage, the Advanced Dressing Station, which is as often as not also pushed right up into the fire zone. The regimental stretcher-bearers therefore begin again another dangerous pilgrimage rearwards.

As there is much ignorance in the public mind on the subject of casualties, it should be well realized that by far the greater proportion of our wounded are slightly hit, and are " walking cases," so little hurt that in innumerable instances where the stretcher-bearers themselves have fallen they have been carried by the slightly wounded soldiers.

I know no more moving experience than an afternoon in an advanced dressing station. Let me describe that of West Péronne. Its location is changed now, so I am giving the enemy no information. We reached it on a heavy and sultry Sunday afternoon by hiding ourselves behind anything possible. Dust and smoke gave the atmosphere of a coming thunder-storm, the thudding of the guns on both sides was incessant. Now and then was heard the brisk note of a machine-gun, which sounds for all the world like a boy rasping a stick along palings or the rattle which policemen carried in Mid-Victorian days.

There was no sign of anything in the nature of a hospital, a tent, or of anything above ground. I was getting somewhat weary of being told to lie down flat every few seconds to avoid bursting shells, when I saw a couple of stretcher-bearers coming through the haze as from nowhere and then disappear underground. "It is underneath *there*," I was told by my guide, whose daily duty it was to inspect these medical outposts.

As quickly as possible we got down into a trench and followed the stretcher-bearers. There, in darkness lit by a few candles, we gradually made out a very grim scene. Talking was difficult, for one of our batteries had just come into action a few yards away.

Owing to the heavy enemy shell fire, what I soon found to be an underground maze—a plan of which appears on next page—had become completely blocked with wounded men lying in the dark on their stretchers, the passage ways dug out of the clayish earth being just the width of a stretcher handle and no more. We trod gently from stretcher handle to stretcher handle over the silent men, some of them asleep with the blessed morphia in their brains, others cheerily smiling, others staring as wounded men do. All who could move a hand had a cigarette— now admitted to be the first need of all but the very dangerously wounded.

Passing on, and using our electric torch as little as possible, so as not to disturb the sleepers, we came to the main dressing room. Remember it was all underground, all dark, and that the oncoming wail of approaching shells, with immediate subsequent explosions, was continuous.

In this main dressing room the doctors, all young men, some of them subalterns of the R.A.M.C., were washing and bandaging with the care and speed that can be seen in the Somme film. I counted twenty-four patients in that small chamber. We crept onward and came to another room where there were nine cases, and again to a smaller one where lay the more dangerously wounded.

These dressing rooms were protected by some four or five feet of earth above them. There was a

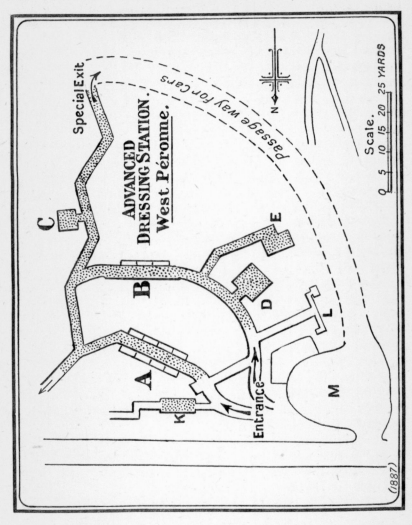

small officers' mess and a medical storeroom, which were merely shielded by corrugated iron from shrapnel splinters, a kitchen, an office, and that was about all. An operation for tracheotomy was taking place in one of the dressing rooms.

In all my many experiences abroad I have never seen a more touching sight than this little underground gathering of some seventy men, devoted doctors and assistants, waiting amidst the incessant shelling until the overcrowded maze could be evacuated. Let those who take their ease on a Sunday afternoon, or any other afternoon, realize that this same scene never ceases. Let those who consider that they are amply doing their " bit " by keeping things going at home be grateful that their " bit " is not as that of these young men. We cannot all of us share the danger, but we can every one of us admit the harsh inequalities of our respective war work.

One or two of the patients were shell-shock victims, and it was piteous to note their tremor at the approaching shell wails and subsequent thuds just outside our little catacomb.

The plan on the opposite page gives a suggestion of the ingenuity with which the R.A.M.C. officers have converted a bit of an old German trench-work to the purposes of an underground hospital and home for the doctors and their assistants.

The shelling increased in intensity. It became obvious that we had to remain concealed till the storm had ceased. In the interval we discussed things about wounded men. We learned that quite a considerable proportion of them had dressed their own wounds with the little first field dressing that is sewn into the tunic of every soldier. Others had got along well enough with the medical help of regimental stretcher-bearers. The rest had been tended at the Regimental Aid Posts to which I have referred.

*   *   *   *   *

Presently the Germans diverted the attention of their gunners to another point of the line, and we were able to emerge into daylight once more and join a small company of lightly wounded and stretcher-bearers on their way to a Walking Wounded Collecting Station. I name all these distinct stages in the progress of the wounded man in order to show how carefully the system has been thought out and organized. It is a tribute to the foresight of our medical authorities that all this vast scheme had been arranged before the war.

On our way rearwards to the Walking Wounded Collecting Station we were passed by some horse-ambulances which, summoned by telephone, were proceeding to the underground hospital we had just left. On our way we escaped the only enemy aeroplane attack that came to my notice during this visit to the front. An officer and a few men were wounded. It speaks eloquently for the celerity with which our casualties are cleared when I tell you that on that same evening, many miles away in the rear, I saw this particular wounded officer sitting in bed nonchalantly enjoying his dinner. By the next day, I was told, he would probably be in England.

The Walking Wounded Collecting Station consisted of marquees in which a considerable number of Tommies of all dialects were partaking of a hearty meal. As each arrived his name and regimental number were entered, with particulars of his case. Where necessary his dressings were re-arranged, and in every case a cigarette was offered. Prodigious quantities of tea, cocoa, soup, bread, butter and jam were disappearing. Despite the bandaged heads and arms of some and the limping of others, they were a merry, if tired, party. Eagerly and in vigorous and unprintable Anglo-Saxon one of them said : " I want to have another smack at the —— Allemans." In a tent was a wounded officer, famous in the world of big game (scarred as the result of a miraculous escape from an African elephant), who, though covered with blood, had only one anxiety, and that was to have his wound dressed, get a bath, and return to his men in time for the next " stunt " —to use an abominable Americanism which has grown weed-like into our war language.   Two days before, this Walking Wounded Collecting Station had been shelled by the enemy.   By a strange stroke of fortune the only victims were a large number of German prisoners.

Life is held gaily and cheaply in these advanced hospitals.   There was a small underground chamber here fitted with bunks as on shipboard, in which the officers could sleep if they chose, but they did not seem to be particular whether they used it or not.

      *   *   *   *   *

We shared the soldiers' meals, listened to their stories—each one of them a full adventure, in peace time—and continued basewards, accompanied by motor ambulances in which sitting cases were carried, to a great Corps Collecting Station, a veritable Clapham Junction of the evacuating system.

To prevent mistakes, each man's label is checked at every point he arrives at with as much care as a registered letter on its way through the post. There is no Red Tape, and nothing is left to chance. There is no lost time.   It is never forgotten that pain is ever present and that saving time may mean saving life.   But even though we have not yet come to that link in the chain—the hospital which is kept neat and burnished by the hand of woman —all is well arranged and spotlessly clean.   Many dressings were being re-examined and many wounds again attended to.

Here I saw the field operating theatre nearest to the battle.   It was in a spotless tent with a table, a powerful acetylene lamp, chloroform, and instruments—all ready. Operations in the field are a rare exception in the British Army. The matter of their necessity has been discussed and re-discussed. There are arguments for and against. But Sir Arthur Sloggett, General Macpherson, and the famous surgeons we have at the front, with Sir Alfred Keogh at home, may be relied upon to know their business to the tips of their fingers. In other armies, notably the Italian, urgent operations take place in what answer to our Advanced Dressing Stations. An Italian officer said to me : " We should not do it unless we had to. Many of our cases would not stand transport from our Alpine heights."

*　*　*　*　*

Resuming our journey with the ambulances, we came, after an hour's halting journey through the dust and the A.S.C. convoys to a Casualty Clearing Station—the first hospital of a kind visualized by the general public.

I have discovered from their conversation that very few people realize the intricate nature of the net spread by the R.A.M.C. over the field of war. The meshes are many—but not too many. An important part of the net are these very perfect clearing establishments. The description of two will be sufficient.

One of these Clearing Stations was a large old water-mill which had been transformed into a most beautiful hospital. I reached it in time to witness the arrival of the ambulances. Out of them came all manner of wounded, British and German. Friend and foe were treated alike. They were just wounded men—that was all. Such as could walk by themselves or with the help of orderlies, came out dazed into the sunlight from the ambulances. The Germans, who had for days been trench-bound by our barrage, were, as a rule, horribly dirty and impossible to approach for physical reasons. Later, at another hospital I saw gently-born V.A.D. nurses washing great unbathed wounded Prussians and Bavarians. I felt positively guilty when I thought of the chaff with which the V.A.D. movement, its uniforms and salutings, was received ten years ago in the bad old days when we ought to have been preparing for war.

Here, in this mill Casualty Clearing Station, the broken soldiers came for the first time under the influence and gentle touch and consoling smile of women nurses. Many of the men had been in and about the firing line for weeks, several of the Germans for longer than that. I talked with some of the enemy who had arrived a day or two before in what must have seemed a fairy palace. Some spoke of the care, kindness, good food, flowers, and music (the gramophone never stops) which were provided. As a rule they are grateful—at any rate at first. Some are very grateful. One officer used the word "lovingly" (liebvoll), and "lovingly" it must seem, for nothing is more marked in inspecting German hospitals, even such an establishment as the Rudolf Virchow Hospital in Berlin, than to notice the roughness of the surgery, the callousness shown in making remarks before patients, and the inferiority of the under-trained nurses.

Some are not grateful and, like the pampered civilians at the Alexandra Palace, think it necessary to place on record complaints based on mere hostility.

This Casualty Clearing Station, placid with its river, with its sunny gardens—into which many beds had been carried so that the wounded might enjoy the birds, the flowers, and trees—seems like an oasis after the grim desolation of the wilderness of the Somme heights.

It is impossible to convey in words the amazing tireless activity of the nurses and doctors. I did not know that human beings could work so many hours without sleep at the most anxious kind of work the world provides. No wonder that the women sometimes break down and require hostels and rest homes. Yet during a number of war visits I have not met with one complaint from any member of any medical staff in the field or elsewhere. There is, on the other hand, the same continuous enthusiasm throughout the medical service as one sees in the great boot factory at Calais, in the vast motor repair shop in Paris, or our transport from Havre to the Front. The stimulus of war seems to double the energy of every human being as soon as he lands in France.

At this great Casualty Clearing Station by the railway the hospital trains were collecting. When we had been shown through the cool tents and had talked with men we happened to know, we went on to the newly made railway platform where the stretchers were being assembled. It was a scene almost of gaiety. The gramophone was playing the inevitable " If You Were the Only Girl in the World." Jokes, cigarettes, and newspapers were passed about. The men looked the acme of content in their beautiful white train. They were willing and anxious to chat. They were interested in all that was going on, and grateful. Many might be going to " Blighty " (Britain), the paradise of the wounded man's imagination.

I do not know whether anyone has written an account of these trains, the doctors and nurses who live in them year in and year out, travelling thousands of miles in the course of a twelvemonth, but someone should do so. My own information is as yet so scanty as to be little worth reading.[1] Of the wonderful hospital barges, too, which, whenever possible, are used on the wide French rivers and canals to carry

---

[1] I have since read with interest a remarkable record, *The Diary of a Nursing Sister* (William Blackwood and Sons).

cases that cannot stand any shaking, not enough
has been said.

It was interesting at the Clearing Station to see
evidence of the Red Cross Society in the existence
of the comfortable English beds of many of the
sufferers. In the world of wounded all sorts of little
things have an importance not understood by the
generality of us. A man likes to lie in bed rather
than on a stretcher not merely for the sake of custom
and comfort. Such is human nature that one man
feels proud of having a bed when another man has
not.

The train took away all in a fit condition for
travel, leaving behind such cases as those of serious
chest, abdominal, and head wounds in the care of
surgeons.

*   *   *   *   *

On a later day I saw the arrival of one such train
at one of those hospitals which look out on the sea
and are situated on the Northern French coast,
which long before the war was recognized as a great
healing place. The medical journals tell their readers
in their own language of these wonderful hospitals
—converted casinos and hotels and miles of perfectly-
equipped huts. Our hospitals in France are a world
of their own. I do not know how many women and
men they employ, but I should say more than one
hundred thousand. In the Etaples district alone
there are 35,000 beds. Canada, Australia, New
Zealand, Newfoundland, India, and the whole of
the Empire have given with both hands.

Those of the wounded who can be made well
quickly enough—and they are, of course, the immense
majority—go back to their war duties at the front,
some eagerly, all without murmuring. As they lie
there in these wonderful huts, in which every provision for speedy convalescence, for happiness, and
reasonable amusement are afforded, tended as they

are by the best surgeons and physicians of the English-speaking world, and by ladies simply and gently born, they all tell you the same story—they would like to get a glimpse of " Blighty " before going back again to fight.

I went on board one of the white hospital ships, marked against submarines on each side with a huge red cross, to see them going home. Arriving on the quay in the British Red Cross and St. John ambulances, and gently carried, with the peculiar, slightly swaying walk of the trained stretcher-bearer, they pass on to the ship and descend in lifts to the particular deck on which is their cot or bed. There can be nothing of the kind in the world better than these speedy, perfectly lit and ventilated vessels.

Once on board, and yet another stage nearer " Blighty " and the beloved ones, all are content-ment itself. Some of the less injured men were on deck singing merrily. Others of the wounded were discussing a newspaper article outlining a project for the settling of soldiers on land in the Dominions after the war. " Many will go to Canda ; some to Australia, I dare say," said one man ; " but I am one of those who mean to have a little bit of ' Blighty ' for myself. We see enough in France to know that a man and his family can manage a bit of land for themselves and live well on it."

I remember a similar conversation a year ago close to Ypres, when a young sergeant, who had been a gamekeeper at home and a working man Conservative, observed, " The men in the dug-outs talk of a good many subjects, but there is one on which they are all agreed. That is the land question. They are not going back as labourers, or as tenants, but as owners. Lots of them have used their eyes and learned much about small farming here."

As I watched the swift ship and saw her speeding away to England at well over twenty knots, I wondered if people and politicians at home are beginning to understand that the bravery and *camaraderie* of the officers and men in the field have broken down all class feeling ; and that our millions of men abroad are changed communities of whose thoughts and aims we know but little.

*　　*　　*　　*　　*

Just as Grant's soldiers, the Grand Army of the Republic, dominated the elections in the United States for a quarter of a century, so will the men I have seen in the trenches and the ambulances come home and demand by their votes the reward of a very changed England—an England they will fashion and share ; an England that is likely to be as much a surprise to the present owners of Capital and leaders of Labour as it may be to the owners of the land.

RED CROSS VISITS

H

I

THE PEOPLE AT 83 PALL MALL AND ELSEWHERE

THE world-wide war work of the British Red Cross Society and Order of St. John of Jerusalem, to which I shall refer, in future, by the generic title of the British Red Cross, ranks among the chief of the achievements of proved British organizing capacity.

Such a far-flung and minutely complicated machine did not spring like Minerva from the head of Jove. It was born amidst the toil and trouble, rush and mismanagement to be expected by a nation caught unprepared. The sudden demands for help from the Red Cross that followed the retreat from Mons were met, expensively perhaps, but they were met. And after all, when the mansion is burning it is no time to haggle about the cost of the fire engine.

My personal connexion with and subsequent intimate knowledge of the British Red Cross followed an appeal for funds issued in *The Times* newspaper, generously and continuously supported by practically every leading journal at home and overseas. I soon found that I was to be held responsible by numbers of donors of sums, great and small, for what they considered to be mismanagement on the Continent. I quickly discovered that givers need and deserve information as to the handling of their moneys. I went abroad to investigate, and made my first acquaintance with the edge of the beginning of the Great Crusade at the time of the Battle of the Marne. When the complaints were analyzed, it was easy to

H 2

see that the evil growths were just the ordinary weeds that spring up in soil long untilled. Most of them were mistakes of the heart and not of the head, and none of the mistakes were very serious. In the first few weeks of the war every individual nerve in the Empire tingled to be doing something. People rushed hither and thither formulating all sorts of schemes, starting all manner of committees ; many dashed across to France and even farther afield in the burning desire to do something.

The British Red Cross promptly took its mistakes in hand, and owing to the indefatigable labours of what became the Joint Committee and its assistants, the present smooth-working, thrifty, responsive and ever-growing organization was soon in being.

Primarily, I take it that the office of the Red Cross is to add just those additions to the medical and relief organizations provided by Government which it is difficult for Government departments to provide quickly. It is the speed with which the Red Cross does things that makes it so valuable an adjunct to the Royal Army Medical Corps and a score of other official organizations.

While every penny is held to strict account, money has been forthcoming on many occasions to the extent of thousands of pounds at the receipt of some vital telegraphic despatch from one or other of the many theatres of war. I shall endeavour to catalogue some of the things the Red Cross does, some of the goods supplied. A veritable army, employing directly and indirectly at least fifty thousand women and men, voluntary and paid, has its well-known headquarters at 83, Pall Mall, where work is carried on by day and by night three hundred and sixty-five days in the year.

The British Red Cross and Order of St. John had the excellent fortune to be assisted from the outset by some of the best organizers in the Empire, as I shall show. When the late Lord Rothschild gave me the opportunity of assisting, he had already around him capable men. The great struggle in France grew, and to these helpers were added the voluntary services of other leading men of affairs, men whose careers at home and overseas were indicative of high administrative capacity.

I have often, of *malice prepense*, suggested to some of my political acquaintances involved in the shortcomings, muddles, miscalculations and underestimations of the first two years of the war, that, had the management been left to 83, Pall Mall and the soldiers and sailors, a good many of the black pages that will stand out in history, and increasingly so as the war is seen in its proper perspective, would not have been written.

I am furthermore of opinion that the addition of feminine insight to the councils of the Red Cross G.H.Q. has had a great deal to do with the absence of that foolish optimism which would have prevented the Red Cross operations being conducted as they are— not for this year or for next year—not for 1916 and for 1917, but, if needs be, for 1918, 1919 : yes, and even for 1920, too.

With the union (for which *The Times* can claim some credit) of the British Red Cross Society and the Order of St. John for the period of the war at least (and as some of us hope for all time) a Joint Committee of the two organizations became a prime necessity.

This Committee was formed and commenced its operations on October 20th, 1914, by which time it had made 83, Pall Mall its G.H.Q. The Chairman of the Joint Committee was, and is, the Hon. Arthur Stanley, C.B., M.V.O., M.P. Mr. Stanley's eldest brother, Lord Derby, has done yeoman service in other fields since the outbreak of war, while all his other brothers are serving either with the Army or Navy with distinction to themselves and benefit to their country.

Mr. Arthur Stanley sits in his office on the third floor of the building in Pall Mall for long hours on every day of the week, and from his office radiate the directions which, as Chairman of the Joint Committee, he issues to every department of the organization. He is the mouthpiece of the Joint Committee, its medium of communication with the Military Authorities, and the mainspring of its inspiration. How much the work of the Red Cross owes to its Chairman will probably never be known, and Mr. Stanley would be the last to wish me to assess it. His sweetness of disposition, and firmness of purpose make him *facile princeps* in the art of smoothing ruffled susceptibilities, masculine and even feminine, of individuals and even of whole Committees. It only remains to be said that, like all his family, Mr. Stanley is a sound and unquestioned Conservative, so far as these party labels have any meaning nowadays.

At the right hand of Mr. Stanley is Sir Robert Hudson. At the outbreak of the war Sir Robert was the Chief Agent of the Liberal Party. When war swept over the world he was permitted by the chieftains of his party to throw up his work, and, for the period of the war, to hang up his hat at the headquarters of the Red Cross, and there he has been practically ever since for ten hours a day and longer.

Sir Robert's nominal title in Pall Mall is Chairman of the Joint Finance Committee. His real vocation is Financial Manager of the Red Cross G.H.Q. A man with five million or more pounds in his keeping needs a strong control of his generous impulses, and Sir Robert possesses it. He has the faculty of saying " No " more agreeably than any friend of mine except Mr. Arthur Stanley. He is fully responsible for success or failure. If anything goes wrong with Red Cross finance, it is he who would be suspended from a lamp-post conveniently situated outside his office in Pall Mall, to which fact his attention is constantly called.

Association with Sir Robert Hudson has taught me a great deal. For a number of years, in common with others of sound political views, I have been engaged in fighting the wicked machinations of the Radical Party in England. I surmise now that the reason of many of our failures was the presence of Sir Robert at the Liberal headquarters. It is reassuring to know that he is a force with whom we shall not have to contend in the immediate future, for his services have been lent to the Red Cross for the period of the war. Certain optimists concerned in our work are flattering themselves that by a process of peaceful persuasion we shall win Sir Robert from his evil political ways. Whether there is foundation for this hope, remains to be seen. He may have a political conscience. But, even if he has, it is permissible to hope that, some day, he may find salvation.

Sir Robert Hudson, who might probably, had he wished it, have been an influence in one of the great departments of State, links up and controls the infinitely complex organization of the Red Cross with a well-concealed hand of iron. I say unhesitatingly that I hope he and Mr. Arthur Stanley and Sir William Garstin (to name only three of them) will remain where they are until war is a thing of the past.

Accustomed myself to a wearisome round of organization, and believing that I understand something of the direction of staffs, I never visit the Red Cross G.H.Q and its numerous and varied offshoots abroad without feeling that any change in the administration at 83, Pall Mall would be a serious blow to a wonderful achievement in efficiency.

The Red Cross has no direct connexion with Government. There are no jobs to be found for office seekers, no rewards are expected or given to the workers. Honours lists pass by unread in the stress of work. Political, social and pecuniary pressure are unknown, though perhaps a little was ineffectually attempted in the early days, before the Stanley–Hudson combination had manifested itself. The true distinction of Red Cross service is that it should pass without "recognition." Even my comments here will, I daresay, be resented by those whom I venture thus to mention.

Sub-Committees of the Joint War Committee have been set up for all the principal branches of the work. The chief of these departments are :—

The Finance Department (which directly affects, and so far as money is concerned, controls every branch of the work),
The Stores and Transport Department,
The Collections Department,
The Motor Ambulance Department,
The Motor Launch and Hospital-Ship Department,
The General *Personnel* Department,
The Medical and Surgical *Personnel* Department,
The Trained Nurses Department,
The V.A.D. Department,
The Auxiliary Home Hospitals Department,
The Convalescent Homes for Officers Department,
The Missing and Wounded Inquiry Department,
The Prisoners of War Department,
The Travelling and Passport Department,
The Hospital Trains Department,
The Anglo-French Hospitals Department,

and there are in addition offices which deal with :—

General Enquiries,
Accountancy,
Pay of *Personnel*,
Contracts for *Personnel*,
King George Hospital,
The " Star and Garter " Home,
Convalescent Camps,

Church Collections,
Issue and Receipt of Collecting Boxes,
Printing and Stationery.

There is a room in which a doctor attends to
medically examine and inoculate the staff proceeding
abroad. There are a telephone exchange, a tea room for
the female staff, typists' and clerks' rooms, a printing
and duplicating room, and scores of other offices
where idleness is unknown. Finally there is a large
chamber which is used for meetings of the important
Committees and Sub-Committees, where alone it is
hinted, by those who do not sit on the Committees,
that time is occasionally wasted.

Apart from the central stores in Pall Mall there are
a variety of other stores in various convenient parts
of London. The Medical and Surgical Stores occupies
a building in Store Street, Tottenham Court Road.
The greater part of Devonshire House, lent by the
Duke and Duchess of Devonshire, is devoted to the
work of the V.A.D., whether of the British Red Cross
Society or of the Order of St. John. 18, Carlton
House Terrace, lent by Lord Astor, is given over to
the work of the Missing and Wounded Department.

Very extensive premises have just been acquired
in Thurloe Place, opposite Brompton Oratory, as the
headquarters of the Prisoners of War Committee,
which will be charged with a regular dispatch of parcels
to all British prisoners of war. Surrey House, Marble
Arch, lent by Lady Battersea, houses the War Library,
which dispatches books, magazines and papers for
the sick and wounded, both at home and abroad.
The Central Workrooms carries on its immense work
in the Royal Academy, thanks to the generosity of
Sir Edward Poynter and the Council.

These are the chief departments which fall under
the immediate control and supervision of G.H.Q.
Farther afield are, of course, the headquarters and

branches of the Joint Committee's activities in France
and Flanders, in Italy, Egypt, Malta, Salonica,
Mesopotamia and India, and British East Africa.
Each of these areas has a Chief Commissioner and
staff of doctors, nurses, accountants, store-keepers,
mechanics, ambulance drivers, orderlies, and clerks.
The Joint Committee has assisted in setting up
hospitals and providing ambulances in Russia and
Roumania. In the Mediterranean and in Eastern
waters it has a fleet of motor boats for the conveyance
both of the wounded and of Red Cross stores and
comforts. Its fleet of ambulances, lorries, repair cars,
soup kitchens, numbers over 2,100. Its vehicular
machinery comprises X-ray cars, dentists' cars, cycles,
wagons, post offices.

Its *personnel* in every branch of its work from doctors
to ambulance drivers is very largely voluntary and
unpaid. The head of every department in England,
and the commissioners and chief officials in all the
theatres of war, are all serving without pay, and even
where pay is drawn there must be innumerable cases
where it represents only a fraction of the income
which the official could have commanded if he had
remained in his ordinary sphere of life.

I could illustrate this by the case of doctors who
at the outbreak of war gave up lucrative practices
bringing them in many thousands a year and " signed
on " with the Red Cross for service abroad at the flat
rate of £1 per day. The pay which they receive would
in many cases be insufficient to meet the rent of their
rooms in Harley Street. It may fairly be said that
every worker under the Red Cross, paid or unpaid,
has made some sacrifice and has made it eagerly and
gladly.

It may be thought that these numberless departments (most of them with a committee of experts to
guide them) with the need of holding numerous meetings of the committee must inevitably produce delay,

but that is not the case. The committees deal with matters of principle, and the ordinary control of the daily work is left to the head of the department and his staff. If the Joint War Committee considers that £50,000 worth of stores, should be dispatched to Mesopotamia, or that a hospital ship, costing £20,000, should be built for the Tigris, and if the Finance Committee approve the expenditure, a notification is made to Sir William Garstin. Sir William, an administrator whose work is known throughout the Empire, was a very fortunate catch for the Red Cross. It is he who presides over the Stores Department. Should the urgent matters concern boat-transport, Mr. George Warre, who has charge of the Motor Launch and Hospital Ship Department, is naturally consulted.

Emergency meetings of many of the Committees are called at a few hours' notice. Most of the members are to be found for ten hours a day at 83, Pall Mall, and not merely a quorum but a full attendance can be ensured at the shortest notice. It is recognized that all the work of the Joint Societies is urgent and that none of it will brook delay. Everything can be found in the Pall Mall building, with the single exception of Red Tape.

It is impossible to exaggerate the debt which the Joint Societies owe to the heads of their various departments. The Stores and Transport Department is, as we have already mentioned, controlled by a great Empire-builder, Sir William Garstin; the Medical and Surgical *personnel* is inspected and chosen by Sir Frederick Treves; the Collections Committee is served by Sir Charles Russell; the Motor Ambulance Department is directed by a man of the great business capacity of Mr. E. M. Clarke; the Auxiliary Home Hospitals Department is under the charge of Dr. Robert Fox-Symons; Sir John Furley (who did Red Cross work in the Franco-

German War of 1870) controls the Hospital Trains Department; the Hon. Reginald Coventry devotes himself to the Travelling and Passport Office; Surgeon-General Sir Benjamin Franklin controls the *personnel* Contract Department; Sir Starr Jameson directs the dispatch of parcels to the Prisoners of War. These men are incalculable assets to the organization.

That alert and hustling monarch, King Manoel of Portugal, a young man with a future, I am very sure, is a tireless Red Cross worker.

I have already hinted that the Red Cross owes much to the women who serve it. Mrs. Charles Furse, the widow of the distinguished painter, is in command of the V.A.D.'s; Miss Swift is Chief Matron of the Trained Nurses' Department; Georgina Lady Dudley manages the Department for Convalescent Officers; Lady Gosford is at the Central Workrooms. These are only a few of those whose names deserve to be remembered in the years to come.

But apart from these heads of departments a tribute must be paid to every worker, paid or unpaid, male or female, of the great army at home and abroad which devotes itself so ungrudgingly to the work of organization. The spirit of sacrifice animates everyone from the highest to the lowest. It is noteworthy that the Boy Scouts of the Red Cross run more quickly on their errands than others do.

The immense daily correspondence at G.H.Q. is opened and dealt with on a most careful system, made necessary by the fact that a large proportion of the letters are either of extreme urgency or contain remittances which require careful accountancy and safe banking and acknowledgment.

When the letters have been opened and docketed, they are circulated to the departments to which they relate, after being recorded in a register and marked so that the actual opener of the letter can always be identified. With remittances running into hundreds of thousands and aggregating nearly £5,000,000, it is a fine testimonial that there is hardly a case of a missing contribution, and in the few cases which have arisen it is almost certain that the loss has been in transmission in the post or has happened, alas ! from time to time, by the destruction of a ship carrying mails from abroad.

By close accountancy, a careful watching of the balances at the bank, and a speedy investment in short term Treasury Bills of all available balances, a sum has been earned in interest which in itself will probably turn out to be sufficiently large to defray the administrative expenses of the Joint Committee in Pall Mall.   This is largely the work of Sir Robert Hudson, and is evidence that the Liberal War Chest, so disturbing to humble Tory workers like myself, is carefully financed.

The Red Cross revenue has been drawn from every part of the King's Dominions, and indeed from sympathizers in many neutral countries, who, if they do not take sides in the world conflict, at least feel for others who are broken in the fight.

It has been the privilege of *The Times* (and its weekly edition) not merely to make the appeal known to the English-speaking world, but also to acknowledge in its columns day by day since August, 1914, the moneys which have been sent in response to the appeal.   In the history of charitable appeals there has never been any such response as that received to the cry of the British Red Cross.   Six thousand pounds a day has been asked for, and for a period of 26 months this average has been steadily maintained and indeed slightly exceeded.

When the first year's accounts of the Joint Committee were published, they were reviewed in the columns of *The Times* by the acknowledged head of the accountants' world, Sir William Plender.   Sir William stated after his examination of the accounts

" that (excluding hospitals) the total home administration and management expenses including the unpacking, sorting, and repacking of gifts in kind only amount to £41,070, equal to 2¼ per cent. of the total income, or approximately 5½d. in the pound. . . . Few administrative bodies are required to meet such unexpected demands upon their resources, or are called upon to cope with so many emergencies as are those controlling Red Cross work.

" The wise and economical administration of public funds calls at all times for the exercise of unusual qualities ; but the difficulties and responsibilities are vastly increased where a great organization has to be built up in a short time during a period of unprecedented commercial and financial disturbance, and to meet demands the nature and extent of which cannot be foreseen.

" That further appeals will be made to the generosity of the public and still heavier calls made on the activities of the Joint Committee cannot be doubted, but if the experience of the past be any guide to the future, no apprehension need be felt on either ground. It must be no little satisfaction to the many thousands of contributors at home and overseas to realize that the work of the Joint Committee—who are trustees for the public—has been worthy of the great task committed to their keeping."

In connexion with the financial side of the work, it is right that recognition should be paid to the debt which the Joint Committee owes to Messrs. Chatteris, Nichols & Co., who act as hon. auditors, and whose staff are always at work, either in England or on the Continent, without receiving any remuneration for the work ; to Messrs. Kemp, Sons, Sendell & Co., who are in charge of the Accountancy Department at Pall Mall ; and to Mr. Basil Mayhew, of Messrs. Barton, Mayhew & Co., chartered accountants, who from the inception of the Joint Finance Committee has acted as its Secretary, and whose services to the Joint Societies are beyond computation.

It is impossible, in such a review as this, to give any idea of the varied activities and energies which a visit to 83, Pall Mall would disclose. The London public are already familiar with the spectacle of a large part of Pall Mall being permanently occupied by the great motor lorries and delivery vans of the Stores Department. The Joint Committee were well advised when they pitched their tent in a thoroughfare like Pall Mall, where the passer-by can see for himself something of the output which ceases neither by day nor by night, and which extends itself over seven days a week.

Just after the assassination at Sarajevo, which Germany made her pretext for the war, I was idling at what is now one of the greatest Red Cross centres and the most important continental base. That beautiful summer of 1914 saw such an upheaval at Boulogne as has not been witnessed since Napoleon encamped his quarter of a million on the same ground where some of our Boulogne and Wimereux hospitals are now placed.

The northern coast of France was beginning to get an unusually good " season." At Wimereux Mr. Hilton had just completed a golf course equal to many of those in East Lothian. The roses at the villas of Le Touquet were in their first glory. Little brown legs were already running in and out of the freakish houses on the splendid sands at Paris Plage. Boulogne-sur-Mer itself was very much what it was when Charles Dickens loved it.

Mr. Merridew, half bookseller, half antiquary, had given me his essay on the English in Boulogne, and we wandered up to see what remains of the house in which Dickens entertained his mid-Victorian circle. I stayed at the old Hotel Christol—now by a freak of fortune the Red Cross G.H.Q. in France. I was

attached to the hotel because of its association with
many happy holidays, and also by reason of the fact
that it was there, far from the madding crowd, and
the observant eye of Fleet Street, that Mr. Moberly
Bell and I concluded the negotiations by which I
became associated with *The Times*. The actual
rooms in which these negotiations took place are now
the centre of one of the most interesting portions of
the work of the Red Cross, the Boulogne branch of
the search for the missing.

But this is no place for peace time reminiscence.
I hurried home as events grew more ominous, and when
I next saw the grey old town it was in the hands of
the Allied forces and the Red Cross had seized my
comfortable hostelry.

    *   *   *   *   *

Let me tell of the men who have done so much for
our wounded at the Chief Foreign Base.

I have pointed out the Red Cross has been fortunate
all through in the manner in which great public
servants were attracted to its cause. At the outset
Sir Alfred Keogh who, with Sir Arthur Sloggett, is
recognized in Allied and even enemy countries as a
great medical organizer, became first Chief Commissioner in France, until, as will be remembered, he was
recalled to England and placed in charge of the medical
service at the War Office. Sir Arthur Sloggett,
genial, alert and shrewd, then succeeded him as
Director-General of the medical service of the British
armies in France, and became at the same time the
titular Chief Commissioner of the Joint Committee
there, the Acting-Commissioner being Sir Savile
Crossley, now Lord Somerleyton.

Next Sir Courtauld Thomson most capably took
things in hand at Boulogne, and when Sir Courtauld
was urgently called East to look after Egypt, Malta,
and the Mediterranean, Sir Arthur Lawley went to
Boulogne and ably continued the chain of notable

administrators. The present Commissioner is the Earl of Donoughmore, who gets through an immense amount of work with much rapidity, and whose Irish sense of humour greatly helps. At the time of writing Mr. E. A. Ridsdale, a Red Cross veteran and known throughout the whole service, is temporary acting Commissioner in France in the absence of Lord Donoughmore, who is trying to settle the differences between the soldiers and politicians in regard to Mesopotamia.

While in Italy I encountered Lord Monson, who is the Italian Commissioner, and whose life is as active as it is interesting. The Commissioners for British East Africa, Mesopotamia, and Salonica are Colonel Montgomery, Colonel Jay Gould, and Mr. Herbert L. Fitzpatrick respectively—all devoted servants of the Red Cross—with many others in distant fields worthy of mention and praise, concerning whom the limits of this book renders it impossible to deal.

The glamour of distance lends enchantment to the idea of Red Cross work abroad. It is glamour and nothing more, for the work is unending and the workers are in exile. But they have their reward, and are probably equally careless of our thanks or of our appreciation.

II

HOW SOME OF THE MONEY IS SPENT.

AT this late period in the history of the War people
are accustomed to take chapters on hospitals as read.
But there is so great a variety in the hospitals of the
British Red Cross Society both as to *locale* and
internal arrangement, that the subject is not so dull
as might be apprehended. First let me say that
in the atmosphere of all the war that I have seen—
British, Canadian, Australian, Belgian, French, and
Italian—there is an activity and eagerness not to
be found, and perhaps not necessary, in hospitals
in peace time. I have no intention of comparing
the merits of hospitals. Hospitals are as jealous
of each other as politicians, generals, or even newspapers. If I dare hint at conspicuous efficiency
there is the Red Cross Hospital at Netley, the
wonderful hospital of the Order of St. John at
Etaples, or any one of the army hospitals at Wimereux
and elsewhere.

Where the staffs of all are animated by so great a
spirit of sacrifice, I will do my best to avoid odious com-
parisons by first describing the British Red Cross
Hospital which, at the time of writing, is still close to
where the shells are falling at Cormons near Gorizia.
All the hospitals that are the occupants of converted
buildings are a testimony to British adaptability and
thoroughness. This hospital at Cormons, which I
have recollections of visiting on a day when the heat
was that of the plains of Hindustan rather than of
Europe, has encased itself in a large and typical

Venetian villa. And our British Red Cross convoys in Italy are our little token of gratitude to our Italian Allies who entered the war in circumstances of extreme difficulty, whose commerce was so enmeshed in the German net, whose aristocracy was so convinced of the invincibility of Germany, whose Vatican was always so apprehensive of the power of Austria. The hospital is staffed, so I was informed, by quite a number of those who have a conscientious objection to shedding blood in warfare. I know nothing of their political opinions, which I did not discuss with them. I was there to examine the efficiency of the hospital. It was the 105th hospital I have entered in the last few years.

Certainly it is most efficient, and if the young men I saw objected to the shedding of blood, they obviously had no objections about assuaging the woes of the blood-bespattered and mangled men who came out of the British Red Cross ambulances from the battle of Gorizia.

As I have pointed out elsewhere in one of the telegrams of which this book is largely composed, the very first person I met coming out of Gorizia and under shell fire which was pouring on the only remaining bridge, was Mr. Trevelyan—one of the heads of this efficient undertaking. If I have a criticism to offer of the British Red Cross Hospital at Cormons on that torrid day, it was that it was overcrowded, but that was not the fault of the hospital, but of the battle. Every possible means had been taken to extend the wards of this old spacious Venetian villa, the outcome of centuries of architectural knowledge and the art of living.

A few days later I had an enthralling afternoon with Professor Boni in his most recent excavations in the Palatine. There, two thousand years old, are the same rooms, the same floorings, the same use of the brilliant red one often found in the shells of

Pompeian houses, that I saw among the mural decorations and in the wall paintings of the large and airy salon at Cormons. To Italian architectural largeness Mr. Trevelyan and his medical associates have added British practical hospital ways. I have recollections of long, perfectly ventilated rooms, the beds filled with bandaged men reading and fanning themselves. Enemy patients were among them, treated, as in every case I have found in Allied hospitals, with as much care as our friends. It made one proud to hear from Italians that this hospital is as close to the firing line as is permitted. It rejoiced me to see our good ambulance drivers running their risk with the same imperturbability as I have seen in the British ambulance drivers at Verdun and elsewhere. Some of the ambulances are now covered with a form of steel network, which may possibly prove some shield against shrapnel splinters, and which undoubtedly gives confidence to the wounded inside. All the arrangements at this hospital are as good as those of our hospitals in France. The difficulties are much greater. Its base is in England. It has to be self-contained in every respect. It has to have its motor repair shop, and supply of spare parts, its own stock of drugs and the other paraphernalia of a war hospital.

I am not an admirer of the type of conscientious objector who prefers the safety of quarry work miles to the rear of where men are never out of danger, but the conscientious objectors, almost entirely members of the Society of Friends, that I have met here and at Dunkirk impressed one favourably. There is not much choice of danger between driving an ambulance in the fire zone and driving an ammunition wagon. Some of the conscientious objectors are quite militant, and one feels that parental or family tradition has a good deal more to do with their opposition than any real objection on their part to

handle a bomb or bayonet. Their avidity for war
news and their keenness in the struggle would, I
think, shock some of the staid folk who sit so mute
and gravely in Meeting Houses at Westminster,
Jordans, or at Germantown, near the City of Brotherly
Love. It is only mere justice to say of the Quakers,
that many of them, at any rate, have done their best in
a very difficult personal situation. They and a host
of other people engaged in the war, including the
regimental doctors and stretcher bearers, officers,
non-commissioned officers and men of the R.A.M.C.,
are officially labelled non-combatants, and are unarmed. Germans in like case, and it is proved
by photographic and other evidence, carry weapons,
if only for self-defence, though I would not have it
deduced that the rifles you may see slung across
the shoulders of the German Red Cross men are
used for aggression. But the only protection our
so-called non-combatants have is their badge, which,
in the excitement, dust and smoke of battle is not a
very powerful protection.

I did not linger unduly at Cormons, because an interesting battle was raging close at hand, and every minute
brought its stretcher with its conscious or unconscious
piece of dishevelled, bloodstained humanity, from which
rose a great cloud of flies—so numerous as to be positively noisy. Inside the hospital there were flies, but
not many. The fight against flies is one of the most
wonderful victories of the hospitals—English and
Italian. At the great Italian base hospital at Udine
the flies seem to have been absolutely vanquished.

*   *   *   *   *

Beyond these remote outposts of the Red Cross
there are others much farther afield, in Salonica,
and Egypt, and farther away than that, which should
be in the thoughts and prayers of the people at home.
There is no going on leave for their staffs—there is nowhere to go. Life is one perpetual round of operations

and of feeding and washing the war victims. At whatever hour of the day or night you may be reading this, remember that in the hospitals all over the world this same noble work is being carried on.

*   *   *   *   *

I have a recollection of another Red Cross hospital, and my recollection is aided by notes kindly provided by Major A. W. A. Irwin, R.A.M.C. It is officially known as No. 2 Red Cross Hospital, Rouen, and its arrangements and the list of the staff give some idea of what is required in a hospital which is, comparatively speaking, by no means one of the largest. Rouen is an interesting centre of British activity abroad. In the days I spent there, there was a permanent English population of over 30,000. There is always a large transient addition to this considerable gathering of men and women, and No. 2 deals with their woes as well as those of the wounded.

In the early days of the War, when the British Expeditionary Force landed on the Continent, among the many buildings and sites of the camps selected in the North of France for hospital purposes was the Grand Seminaire, Rouen. Curiously enough, this was used similarly by the Germans during the Franco-Prussian War.

The Seminaire is a comparatively modern three-storied brick and stone building standing on the hillside overlooking the city, and comprising the main quarters of the priests and students, with their classrooms, libraries, and infirmary under the same roof, and chapel adjoining, together with a detached house of considerable accommodation, a laundry, and outhouses in various corners of the extensive orchards and gardens.

Whilst preparations were being made by the Army authorities to convert this into a hospital, the enemy advanced to within a few miles, and it became necessary to evacuate. After a few weeks, however, the tide had turned sufficiently to allow the city to be reoccupied and work resumed, but instead of carrying out the original intention that the hospital should be purely military, the enterprise of the British Red Cross Society was called upon, and this organization was henceforward mainly responsible for the internal management and expense, running it as a part of the Army—as indeed in this critical and busy time they are running so many similar ventures, the value of which will probably never be fully estimated.

Upon the taking over of the unit which occurred early in September, 1914, several aid posts and rest stations at the neighbouring villages and railway stations were opened and attached.

The original *personnel* consisted of about sixty medical officers, sisters and orderlies in all, who were sent out by the British Red Cross Society from England to be placed under a regular R.A.M.C. Commandant. This staff became modified in various ways according to requirements, the strength for normal working being finally fixed to include the Commandant—a regular R.A.M.C. officer of the Army —6 medical officers, 1 quartermaster, matron and 32 sisters, 35 V.A.D. nurses (including housekeeper), 76 N.C.O.'s and men of all duties, comprising dispenser, radiographer, theatre attendants, male nurse, ward orderlies, clerical staff, storekeepers, plumber, carpenter, cooks, motor lorry driver, gate police, postman, and pioneers, together with 4 Boy Scouts for messenger and general duties. All of these are B.R.C.S. workers, except the Commandant, sergt-major, and 2 N.C.O.'s, who are regular R.A.M.C. men, not paid by the Society, the duties of the latter chiefly lying in dealing with official Army Returns and Statistics.

After the calling up and replacement of eligibles for military service, the whole male *personnel*, except an irreducible minimum of skilled indispensable men, are physically unfit for the army, or not of military age.

By the strenuous and incessant work of the original unit which came out, and that of Royal Engineers, the Seminaire was rapidly adapted for hospital use, and the detached building formed into the home for the staff.

While this was being done, large numbers of wounded were already passing through, the first convoy being admitted on the 26th September, 1914.

In the winter of 1914–15, the accommodation being insufficient for the growing needs, two asbestos huts of the usual Army pattern were set up in the cloistered quadrangle of the main building, holding about twenty beds each, and with these the number of beds was increased to 178 as the normal figure ; in busy times, however, this has been swelled into as many as 250, by the placing of additional beds in the wards and corridors.

The nursing accommodation consists of two large and two small wards of 28, 24, 8 and 7 beds respectively, and two huts holding 20 and 16 beds, besides which there are 90 student rooms, each holding two beds, except on one floor which is primarily reserved for Field Officers. A number of these rooms are used for staff and other purposes, leaving their capacity for patients at 73, giving a total of 176 as the normal number of beds.

In many cases beds are named by donors to the funds of the Society, and the two large wards are now named " The English Public Schools Wards," these schools contributing largely to their main-tenance.

The departments of the hospital are of the usual numerous and varied character, comprising amongst others a large, well-lit and equipped operating theatre with anæsthetising, sterilizing, and X-ray rooms adjoining. Next to these is the dispensary and out-patients' department, in the latter of which cases coming up from the base are examined and treated. The X-ray apparatus was the gift to the hospital by the firm of Ellimans' Embrocation.

There is also a pathological laboratory in which much important work is carried on by an expert bacteriologist, and a room equipped for massage and general electrical treatment.

Slighter cases, who are able to move about, mess in a large and handsomely furnished room—formerly the Seminaire infirmary for sick priests and students. Through this room is a broad balcony covered by a glass awning, forming an ideal sun-room for patients, and looking across the garden with a magnificent view of the cathedral and city, backed on the other bank of the river by tracts of forest land that stretch far away over the distant horizon. Under this balcony is a long arched verandah which serves a like purpose for the lower floor.

The cooking of the hospital is done in the main kitchen, which being designed and furnished for the ordinary needs of the establishment in time of peace, is amply capable of catering for the maximum number of patients in hospital. Three other kitchens serve the home, N.C.O.'s and orderlies' messes.

Placed in convenient parts of the main buildings and outhouses are the stores for linen, rations, meat, coal, patients' kits, quartermaster's stores, and surgical necessaries, as well as the dairy, and a branch of the Expeditionary Force canteens. In the grounds also are the disinfector and incinerator, which play a large part in the general sanitation and health of a war hospital.

The orderly staff are billeted in marquees, Alwyn huts, and buildings in a part of the grounds picturesquely laid out, and sloping up to a stone terrace upon which some of the huts are pitched.

For the first three months of 1915, both officers and other ranks were treated, but subsequently the hospital was reserved for officers only.   In October the hospital was inspected by the King during his visit to the Armies in France.

No change of importance took place until November, when about thirty V.A.D. nurses were sent out, and the male orderly staff reduced—it is hardly necessary to say that the splendid work of these ladies ever since has been of very great value.

During the whole of the two years, the disposition of the French in their capacity of landlords has been not only consistently courteous, but exceedingly generous, and the fact that the late and present Archbishops of Rouen have resided in the château overlooking the hospital has always been one of considerable benefit ; each of these in turn allowing free use of his private grounds and orchard which run up to the door of the palace—a gift which proved of the greatest value for rest and convalescent exercise of the patients—besides which the nave of the chapel is given over, and services are regularly held there by the resident chaplain.

Since its opening, the hospital has treated in round figures a total of 10,000 cases, all of whom were British officers, except some 526 British N.C.O.'s and men, 60 nursing Sisters, 6 patients of French and other nationalities, and one German officer.

The busiest period in its history was the six weeks ending the 12th of August, 1916, during which time 350 operations in the theatre were performed, as well as 300 dressings done under anæsthetics, and 590 X-ray examinations made—a heavy share of work, which was duly commended by the authorities.

Of the original staff which came out in September, 1914, only one Sister remains with the unit, though several others are still working in France.   Their places, however, have been filled from time to time

by the most skilled and well chosen workers, so that
no unit can show a better record. Never in its
history has the hospital been more highly efficient
than at the present time, everything being done to
give the British officer the best possible treatment
and to make him as comfortable as possible.

III

THE SEARCH FOR THE MISSING.

In the earliest days of the War a beloved only son was missing, and his mother asked *The Times* if it could use its organization in Paris to search the battlefields for news of him. One of the members of the French staff of the newspaper spent some three weeks in a vain endeavour to obtain definite information. That, I believe, was the first systematic attempt at what has now grown to be a very important branch of Red Cross work.

Shortly afterwards Lord Robert Cecil went to Paris, and I remember finding him busily at work in a small room in the Hotel Iena. The Department inaugurated by Lord Robert has now become one of the many useful branches of Red Cross work. Lord Robert easily set the example of thoroughness for which the department is known, for he himself went out personally to search cottages and châteaux for men who might have been carried there for treatment, and to discover, if possible, the whereabouts of the graves of the fallen.

The news of this errand of mercy which the Red Cross Society was speeding travelled swift and far, and soon the calls made upon the staff available threatened to overwhelm it. The small effort, it was clear, must be extended—for the idea of abandoning it was not entertained. So larger premises were secured and branches were opened in Boulogne and other suitable places, and a central office was organized in London. Here a large number of charitably minded people laboured to carry on the great mass of work which waited upon their efforts. So fast did the organization grow that the original accommodation at 83 Pall Mall proved quite inadequate. Lord Salisbury then provided larger quarters at 20 Arlington Street, and in February, 1915, the staff was transferred there.

In July, however, more room had become necessary, and then the Duke of Norfolk placed the first floor of Norfolk House at the disposal of the workers. A month later this space was inadequate, and the prisoners' department was transferred to London House. Finally, Lord Astor lent his house in Carlton House Terrace, and there the organization is now housed. The prisoners' department has been constituted now as a separate system.

These quick changes of home reveal clearly how strong a hold upon the public imagination the new work obtained, and how eager all those who had ceased to hear from their friends in France, or who knew that their friends were among the missing, were to avail themselves of help. They reveal also how thoroughly the organization won the public trust, how efficient it was even at the beginning, and how great a want was supplied by it.

The principle of working had, of course, to be evolved, and the difficulties encountered in the course of this work were very many. The first searchers found themselves with a list of names, and with the whole of war-wracked France in which to search for those men. How were they to begin to search? Where were they to go? The armies were fully engaged in battles upon the issue of which hung the fate of Europe; men had small leisure to spare for seeking for fallen comrades.

It was seen that the first step must be to tap the resources of the hospitals. Members of the first little party with which Lord Robert Cecil was identified began to try to gain news of the missing by questioning the wounded. Sometimes this method led to nothing, but frequently a man would be found who had known the lost soldier and marked his fate. In those cases the anxieties aroused were answered at once, and fears and hopes set at rest; in these cases, too, an indication was given as to where the soldier had fallen, if he was dead, so that steps could be taken to mark his burial place.

This identification of graves was carried on until the end of 1914, when it ceased to be part of the duty of the department, the War Office having appointed a Graves Registration Commission under Brigadier-General Fabian Ware. A close connexion, however, subsists between the Commission and the Red Cross Department.

It was an obvious step from this to instal "watchers" in all hospitals. These watchers were given lists of names of missing men, and it was their duty to ask new patients if they knew of anything of these men, to note down their answers and to forward them to headquarters.

On my last visit to Boulogne I spent a morning examining the organization of a hospital ship, and was especially attracted to the work of a searcher— a Roman Catholic priest, the member of a well-known family—who, note-book in hand, was interrogating group after group of the lightly wounded on their way to " Blighty." He very kindly showed me the result of his morning's work, and it occurred to me then that the public might care to read a selection of these war dramas in miniature. At the end of this chapter I have appended a few that tell their own story, in the official language of the reporter, and also in the simple words of the bereaved.

This system formed the backbone of the whole organization, and upon this system the organization is based at the present day. As a system it has been brought to great perfection; every fragment of information is collected; the information is sent out in language which can be understood by the least educated and by those who are bewildered by sorrow. Moreover, testimonials to the daring and devotion of the fallen are gathered, to their endurance under suffering, and to the manner in which their comrades risked and even lost their lives to save them from suffering, death or captivity. No letter, however trivial, remains unanswered; no enquiry, however difficult, is neglected.

Some of the tributes sent by comrades are documents of strange appeal.

" Lieutenant —— " wrote a private in his regiment, " was acting fine. The regiment went on about 20 yards from where he fell and took cover. Private —— got permission to go back to him and take his identity disk and his revolver."

" Your brother," wrote another soldier, " was a grand officer; his men would have followed him anywhere. He fell in the thick of it." And an officer wrote of one of his men, " He was a hero; he was an example to all of us." It is not difficult to understand how these simple expressions written by comrades who have shared the same dangers bring a measure of consolation to the fathers and mothers of our heroic dead.

Each enquiry is filed separately and becomes soon a *dossier*; the moment any piece of information is received by the Bureau it is transmitted to the friends of the soldier. These *dossiers* are human documents of rare interest which none can read unmoved; they reveal, too, in convincing fashion the extraordinary amount of care and thought which is expended upon the work of tracing and searching for the missing. Indeed in this organization is to be found the newest and noblest form of detective enterprise, as full of thrills and surprises, of close deductive reasoning and resourceful cleverness as the memoirs of Sherlock Holmes.

Here, for example, is a case selected at random from among the hundreds, nay thousands, which have been filed. The missing man may be called Private Smith. On the 1st of October, 1915, the Bureau received the following letter concerning him :—

> I should feel most thankful to you if you could possibly trace any news of my dear son reported " Missing " at the Dardanelles in August. I have tried myself but failed.

The enquiry was put in hand at once, and Private Smith's name added to the hospital lists. But on December 13th the desired information was still lacking. Nevertheless it was possible to report :—

> Private Roberts now in hospital abroad states that about 3 days after the landing they were advancing across a plain to go to the first line trenches when the Turks opened fire on them. Our informant was with your son until they had crossed the plain but did not see him fall. The stretcher-bearers never found him, and it was probable, therefore, that he had crawled into the long grass and so got out of sight. If this account is accurate it seems to suggest that your son has been made a prisoner by the Turks, and in this hope and belief we are continuing to make every possible enquiry with regard to the matter, and will at once communicate with you if any further or more reassuring news comes to hand.

The reply to this letter shows how much relief it brought to the boy's mother ; she wrote :—

> I received your welcome letter. I am very grateful to you. I can assure you I shall wait

K

very anxiously for any fresh news of my dear
son, who seems to have been spirited away from
me.

The next letter the mother received was dated
December 22nd. It ran :— .

We have received information stating that
Private X., who was taken to X Hospital, would
be able to give you information about your son.

Then on January 4th, the Bureau wrote further :—

We have received another report which tends
to confirm the possibility of your son having
been taken prisoner by the Turks. Private Y
states as follows :—" I was a machine-gun driver.
We were ordered to advance, to take up a fresh
position in the centre at Suvla Bay. The
sergeant and Smith got too far. Two were
wounded and the gun and two tripods were lost,
and we were ordered to retire. The ground
which was open was occupied by the Turks.
I went out again by daylight, and also by night,
but could find no trace of the sergeant or Smith.
I believe they were taken prisoners. I knew
Smith well ; he came from ——, was of medium
height, and clean-shaven."

The evidence seemed now to be tending to the
prisoner of war theory, but still a great load of
anxiety lay on the mother's mind. After seeing her
son's friend in hospital and receiving this letter, she
wrote: " It seems a number of people saw him up to a
certain point and then missed him, which leaves a
terrible doubt as to whether he was killed or taken
prisoner."

Confirmation of the reports already given was
received in February in the shape of another statement, but the Bureau added : " Up to the present,

however, we have not been able to obtain confirmation of these statements either from the list of prisoners which have reached us so far from Turkey, or from any other source."

This letter was acknowledged with deepest thankfulness. Then came a bitter blow in the shape of another statement.

> They were nearly surrounded. Two were known to have been killed. One of them was missing at the time, but was found two months later in Malta. I believe he had been left for dead, but eventually crawled into the Cheshire lines. Another was said to have been wounded in the wrist, but has disappeared and so has Smith.

The outlook was now black indeed. In April, after receiving a further statement, the Bureau wrote to the soldier's mother :

> We are afraid that there is now little chance of your son being a prisoner, as we should have expected to have received his name in some of the lists which have reached us from Turkey. If, however, there are any other enquiries you would like us to make for you, you have only to let us know. In the meantime we beg once again to assure you of our deep sympathy in the matter.

No definite information perhaps, but how much better than the utter silence which had baffled the seeker before the Red Cross came to her help. At least she was able to picture the last hours of her gallant boy and to be with him in spirit during the moments of his devotion and sacrifice. Nor did the tragic courage of the words in her last letter to the Bureau " I am hoping still " express in any degree a diminution of the gratitude which she felt and acknowledged.

K 2

Many of these *dossiers*, unhappily, tell only a story of sorrow ; there are other cases, however, in which the miracle longed for so eagerly actually happens, and the lost one is discovered. But it must be remembered that appeal is not made to the Bureau until the official sources have been carefully canvassed and other means have failed. In other words, the enquiry in most cases is directed to discovering either in what circumstances a man came by his death, or whether it is possible that he may be a prisoner of war.

Another case, which affords a good illustration of the kind of work being carried on day by day, was first brought to the Bureau's notice in April of this year by a report from the War Office that Sergeant James was missing. " Anything," wrote his wife in asking for help, " would be better than this awful suspense."

Some fifteen days later the Bureau was in possession of information which left little or no doubt that the poor fellow was killed. " An officer," they wrote, " says that during the unsuccessful attack on ——, as he himself lay wounded on the ground, Sergeant James came up and spoke to him ; and that instant the sergeant was very badly wounded in the chest. The officer feared at the time that your husband was killed, but just at this moment the retreat was ordered and the fallen were left on the spot." Further, a private gave the same account and adds that " from the sudden way in which your husband fell he was instantly killed. It was," he declares, " within 10 yards of the German lines about 4 a.m., and bright moonlight. I saw him plainly ; he was my own sergeant."

The poor wife, to whom the names of the informants were given, verified the story herself in a few days, and wrote to the Bureau :

Words simply cannot express my thanks for the kindness and attention you have taken on my behalf. I am indeed grateful. I am positively sure that if it had not been for you I should still be suffering in suspense.

A certificate of her husband's gallantry was afterwards sent to her.

The gratitude of these stricken men and women for the help given them is one of the most wonderful features of this work. It is equalled in its beauty only by the courage and resignation which are displayed. A poor wife who was unable to obtain exact information wrote :

I am broken-hearted at having to confess that I have tried my very best to find him and have failed. So I shall have to place all my trust in our Heavenly Father and wait. When the war is over he may come back to me along with others of our dear, brave men whose wives and mothers have not allowed their fears to quench their hope. I thank you with all my heart, and I pray that God will be with you and the good work you are doing.

Even more touching is this cry of pain, stifled in the uttering : " I am very grateful ; but, oh it is a bitter end to the long, long hoping." And this : " We accept, knowing that he did his duty."

The desire for assurance that the dead man has found a grave, and that his grave is being tended, is also constantly being expressed, and there is a whole world of pathos in the reply of a mother who had received a description of her son's burial place. " We are all glad to know that he lies comfortable."

It is an inspiring thought that this splendid work of seeking is carried out almost entirely by voluntary means. How much the success of it is due to Lord Robert Cecil's early work has already been indicated.

Not less important was the work carried on by Sir Louis Mallet, who during many months presided over the Bureau in London. Sir Louis has now resigned and Lord Lucan has taken up the task.

It has sometimes been asked why this work is carried out by an agency like the Red Cross and not by the War Office itself. The answer is, clearly, that no department of State could hope to touch the human chord which gives this work its greatest value. It would be wrong to expect an already overworked War Office to busy itself collecting small personal details, yet it is just these details for which all those who have suffered the great loss yearn so wistfully. That they should have this comfort is surely beyond all dispute. Who, for example, would deny to a mother a letter like this :

> We called him " Tom " ; he was a dear good fellow. It happened on the left. I saw him fall. So far as I could see, it was all over. He himself said " I am done for ; go on, lads." The ground where this happened was in our possession when I left.

Indeed, the mother's reply furnishes the complete justification for the work being accomplished. " We have heard nothing more from the War Office ; only that he was wounded and missing, and but for your help and kindness we should still be waiting in suspense."

Here are the complete *dossiers* :

THE DOSSIER OF PTE. J. L. D—— OF THE 2ND BLACK WATCH.

I.

28th July, 1916.

Could you possibly find out for me the fate of enclosed soldier, Pte. J. L. D——, 2nd Black

Watch, Indian Expeditionary Force? He was wounded on January 21st in the Persian Gulf. I am enquiring for the family.

M—— H——. (Lady H.)

II.

11th August, 1916.

We have only received one report as to the above, which we now send on to you though we consider it most unlikely to be true, as Pte. D——'s name is not in any list of Turkish prisoners yet received. The report comes from Pte. J. R. ——, 2nd Black Watch, and is as follows :—

" On 21st January, 1916, in Mesopotamia I saw D—— in the Turkish 1st line captured, but trying to get away and calling out, so that he is probably a prisoner of war. The English took the position, but had to retire for lack of reinforcements."

We are continuing enquiries in the hope of gaining more satisfactory information.

To Lady H——.

III.

26th September, 1916.

It is with great pleasure that we can now send you the news that Pte. D—— is a released prisoner of war and has been invalided to India. We had heard nothing beyond the report sent to you on the 11th August, which we hesitated to believe. This good news has come to us from Basra to-day.

Letters to Pte. D—— should be addressed with full regimental particulars, c/o " Casualties,"

Bombay, and the envelope should be marked in the corner " Exchanged Prisoner of War."

We shall be greatly obliged if you will let us know whether Pte. D——'s relatives had had any intimation that he was a prisoner of war, and whether he had been able to communicate with them. Such knowledge, if you can kindly supply it, may be of the greatest assistance to us in comforting other anxious relatives.

To Lady H——.

IV.

9th October, 1916.

Pte. D——'s friends have not heard from him at all, so that they were very grateful for your letter and his address. Thank you so much for your kind help.

Yours truly,

M—— H——.

V.

13th October, 1916.

Lady H—— has made enquiry about my husband, Pte. J. L. D——, 2nd Black Watch. I am very pleased to here the news of him. I heard from the Office at Perth that he was a released Pris. of War, and the 2nd of Oct. I heard again that he as a gunshot wound in the head and heel, and he is at Colaba War Hospital, Bombay, India. I should like to here from him. I have only had one card from him since he was wounded, and that was to say he was at Bagdad. The last letter he wrote was the 16th of Jan. and he was wounded on the 21st Jan. so its nine months he has been wounded I do hope he is getting better I have only seen him once in the two years and I have lost my Brother and Father since he as been away so I have had a great worry and I have three little cheildren so I do hope he will be spared to see them again. I wonder if he is too ill to write as I have not heard from him, and do you think he would be able to come home if he is well enough and would you be able to let me know if he is badly wounded as I am very anxious to know after such a long time. I should be greatly oblige.

E. D——.

VI.

16th October, 1916.

Your letter of the 13th crossed ours to Lady H——. Probably by this time you will have received the very cheering account of your husband which we have sent to her for you. We told her that we had received a report through the War Office that Pte. D—— was in Colaba War Hospital, Bombay, that his wound was healed and his condition good.

This will comfort you very much as he is evidently progressing really well. We do not know what his movements will be, but if we should hear at any time that he has left India, we will let you know.

With many congratulations,

To Mrs. E. D——.

The Dossier of Flight Sub-Lieutenant C. G of the Royal Naval Air Service.

I.

To G. H. G., Esq.

July 18th, 1916.

With reference to your enquiry for Flight Sub-Lt. C. G., Royal Naval Air Service, we have received the following report from Flight Sub-Lt. E——, now in hospital at Bombay, who states :—

" About the 20th April, G—— went up carrying food to Kut. He was attacked by a German machine. His observer was shot dead, and G—— had to land in Turkish trenches, and was made a Prisoner. The Turks sent for his valise and box to Orah and reported that he is well though slightly wounded."

We have not received Flight Sub-Lt. G——'s name on any Prisoners' List yet, but we will inform you as soon as we do so. Prisoners generally are not able to communicate with their relations for about the first four months.

II.

July 27th, 1916.

We beg to send you a further report which we have received about Mr. G——. Our informant, who is now in hospital at Alexandria, states :—

" I saw Mr. G—— start on the 24th to carry food to our chaps in Kut, taking with him as observer, Lt. F——, from the Norfolks. As they passed over the Turkish lines they were attacked by a Fritz (Turkish or German aeroplane), the observer was killed and Mr. G——, who was fired at continuously, was brought down. Either that day or the next, the Turks sent a message by Flag of Truce to Commander B—— that Mr. G—— was wounded and wanted his kit. Everything he had was accordingly sent up stream by motor boat to a place agreed on where the Turks met it. Commander B—— is now at Zanzibar, East Africa. The records have probably gone to England. Mr. G—— was a most enthusiastic pilot, and when he could would go over with food three or four times a day. It was no place for seaplanes, and I remember him saying the Turks would get him soon, before it actually happened."

This is a more detailed account than the last we sent you and tends to confirm that report, and we very much hope that when we obtain full lists of the prisoners in the hands of the Turks we shall find his name in them.

Assuring you of our sincere sympathy in your anxiety.

III.

July 28th, 1916.

I beg to thank you for your letter of yesterday's date giving me much interesting information regarding my son, which has been communicated to you by A. J——, R.N.A.S. You have been most kind in all your efforts in my interest, and I tender my thanks to all those who work so unselfishly for others.

Will you please accept the enclosed £25 as a second donation to your funds from Mrs. E. M. G.?

Yours faithfully,

G. H. G——.

IV.

12. ix. 16.

I have much pleasure in informing you that Flight Lt. C. B. G—— has been released by the Turks.

He has cabled from Amara under date 10th

September that he has been exchanged and is well in health.

Thanking you for your kind efforts on his behalf.

G. H. G——

V.

September 14th, 1916.

We are so glad to hear that you have had a cable from your son, Flight Sub-Lieutenant C. G——, Royal Naval Air Service.

We have also heard from our Office at Basra and were on the point of writing to you to say that we had heard that he was an exchanged Prisoner of War from Baghdad, was quite well, and sailed for India in the Hospital ship *Varsova* on September 10th.

We do indeed congratulate you.

This, then, is a labour of love, belonging in its essence to Red Cross work as that work has come to be understood throughout our land. It is a labour which eases the sorest wounds of warfare and which indirectly brings great comfort to the fighting men themselves, many of whom are haunted by the fear of being numbered among the lost and so becoming a source of suffering to their friends.

The British soldier needs no advertisement, but it is not possible to close this chapter without placing on record the great help which all ranks of the Army give to the searchers for information about the missing. No trouble is grudged by these men if it is likely to help to relieve the burden of their comrades' womenfolk. The wounded in hospitals, indeed, seem to forget their own pains on the instant when this appeal is made to them. Many a sore heart owes its consoling to the action of these splendid fellows ; and many a wife and mother treasures to-day as a priceless heritage the letters written by them in memory of a fallen friend. " I thought perhaps you might like to hear "—the letters often begin, and the note of apology frequently runs all through them. It is the way of the British soldier ; for within the breast of a hero he cherishes ever the heart of a little child.

LIFE IN REIMS

LIFE IN REIMS

The Sign that will be Kept for Ever

REIMS.

As our motor sped toward the stricken town this sunny afternoon, and we got our first view of the two towers of the great church, we rejoiced not a little that, at a distance of a mile, all looked as it did before the Germans came, and when we reached Reims itself there were not, at that particular entrance gate, many signs of change. We were glad to be away from war for a while and to see women and children. For hours soldiers clad in horizon blue, with their paler blue helmets, had been our only companions. Mighty motor-lorries, vast collections of forage wagons, travelling kitchens, automobile searchlights, and the rest of the apparatus of war had blocked the roads for many leagues. In the city itself, except for shut shops as on Sunday, and a look of desolation, our first impressions were that the story of Reims had been exaggerated.

But suddenly, on our way to the cathedral, in the Boulevard de la Paix, strangely named, there were whole mansions down and others so mutilated that they exposed the long-kept privacy of chandeliered *salons*, bedrooms now wrecked, and hanging staircases. It was in the little square in front of the cathedral that we found *Kultur* displayed in its horrid nakedness. The Archbishop's palace looks like a house in Pompeii, the cathedral's face, partly sandbagged, is ruined.

L

Perhaps my readers have known and loved Reims, and can recall the scene at the great west entrance. There is a humble little equestrian figure of Jeanne d'Arc, carrying now in her hand a French flag and decorated around the plinth with many tributes from passing soldiery, who have paused to note the marvel of the fact that her sanctity has not been disturbed by even one shell fragment. To the right of this little figure of Joan the Maid and facing the cathedral is the Hotel of the Lion d'Or, the front damaged, but the house itself, though within a child's stonethrow of the cathedral, hardly hurt. To-day the hotel, reminiscent of the happy holidays of thousands of English and American tourists, bears itself bravely. There were even a few daffodils in the *salle à manger*, and there is a comfortable dug-out below stairs. There was exactly one foreign visitor who shared with us the excellent meal provided—Mr. Frank Hedges Butler, a well-known friend of France and one of the pioneers of the automobile. Here at Reims, with the Huns almost within rifle shot, and in places even more closely adjoining the firing line, the French provide wonderful meals.

I was asked to perform one little act of justice in connexion with the hotel. It is held by Mme. Pfister. Her foreign-looking name gave rise to ridiculous rumours that from the hotel signals were sent to the Hun artillery whereby the hotel was spared and the cathedral shelled. Mme. Pfister is French and her son is in the trenches. When the golden tide of English and American tourists returns every franc will be needed to pay for the devastation sustained, and no unjust slur should deprive this hotel of even one possible patron.

Reims is bombarded with persistent regularity. Its stricken folk are subject to attacks vastly more serious than any Zeppelin raid, and so often that the French *communiques* have ceased to report them. The world outcry has saved the remains of the cathedral.

Let us take a little turn in the town while the guardian of the locked church is fetched. We find that quite a number of people of all classes remain. The old men and women that one associates with war are seated in the doorways of such houses as are not closed or in ruins, children play in the streets their shrill and merry games, a funeral passes with its little procession following. Here and there whole streets are closed, while in others a superficial observer would imagine that life in Reims was going on as usual. Judging by the wall advertisements, there seem to be some amusements, such as kinematographs. There is no lack of excellent food in the shops that are open. The people seem quite undisturbed by the continual murmur of cannon, and indeed after a few minutes one is oblivious of it.

Reims is a queer but quite an attractive *mélange*, difficult to describe. Almost everyone carries a gas mask ; the men keep theirs in compact tin cases slung from the wrist or attached to bicycle handle, the women in various kinds of bags. These masks can be bought at any chemist's and are so prepared as to need merely damping with water when required. The preponderance of the remaining native population is, of course, feminine, mostly workgirls who work in the great champagne *caves*, and in this matter I am asked to state that the war vintage of 1915 is believed to be the best since 1900. Here, deep down underground, thousands of women are busy filling and turning the acres of bottles that are arranged in the wonderful subterranean highways.

We obtained permission to descend into the famous Pommery cellars, which are laid out in what are really streets of wine, the whole forming an underground city of considerable extent. Millions of

bottles are twisted by a dexterous movement of the
hand each day. The process of preparing the champagne
which will one day sparkle on distant tables wherever
there is merriment is so complicated that the relatively
high cost of this wine can be easily understood.
The Remois are highly indignant at letters that
have appeared in the Press advocating the removal
of French wines from British tables. One of them
remarked, " There are the bombs of the Boches over
us by night, and one reads in our newspapers by day
of the economic bombs of John Bull, safe in his
island."

We have not time to tarry in the deep chalk
streets of wine, many of which are named after
American and English cities, such as Manchester-
street, Liverpool-street, New York-street, and the
rest, for Notre Dame is our aim. We have made a
long journey to see it, and we are unfortunate to
have found its guardian away. When we emerge
to the surface and to sunlight and the sound of
guns, we hasten to the cathedral so as to be there
at the appointed moment, when what remains of
the great window will be at its best in the setting
sun. We are amused, *en passant*, by a glimpse of a
real Parisian *élégante*, with the extremely high hat
of the moment, the wide skirt, and the showy boots,
carrying in her right hand her Pekinese and in her
left her gas mask, looking as though she had just
walked in from the Avenue du Bois. A truly remarkable sex !

The people of Reims keep the shell of the cathedral
strictly closed, as though to hide its humiliation
from such few soldier travellers in the war zone
as have time to pause a moment in their urgent and
bloody business. First, after glancing at the ruined
façade, whose graven figures were considered one
of the masterpieces of their period, we pondered some
minutes in the remains of the Archbishop's palace.

We had known it in happier days. The beautiful Salle du Tau, where the coronation banquets were held, had a wonderful fifteenth-century chimney, but nothing remains to-day of the Archbishop's palace but wreckage and blackened and ruined walls. Modern artillery is mathematically accurate. For some fiendish reason the palace had been especially chosen as an objective. It is a building of only two storeys, so low as to be of no possible value as an observation post. The guardian told us that over a thousand shells fell therein.

We passed by a little door into the great church, whose doors had been continuously open since the rebuilding in 1481, and whose walls had contained so much magnificence in the past. Generations of affectionate guardians have seen to it that the coronation place of kings was swept and garnished each day. Now, save for the wild pigeons who are taking up their residence and whose peaceful cooing mingles strangely with the distant booming of German guns, it is bereft of life. The warm scent of incense is gone. The whole vast space of the cathedral, which looks so much bigger than it did before so much of the internal woodwork was burned, is desolation itself. An attempt had been made at a tidying up, and the little, old guardian who shows us the ruins, indicating the obvious deliberation with which various parts of the cathedral have been shelled, tells us that very soon all will be restored and well. He has the absolute confidence of practically every Frenchman we met that the barbarians will soon leave France. He tells us with delight that the famous tapestries, which will be remembered by all, were taken away at the first news of the invasion of the Huns and are safe, as is also, we found afterwards, the beautiful Church of St. Remi.

Many people ask about the glass of Reims and what has happened to it. Much of it is gone. A great deal of it is passing over the world in fragments as souvenirs. Set in the aluminium rings made in the trenches from German fuzes, the blue glass is difficult to distinguish from sapphire.

As the moment came for saying farewell to Notre Dame the great rose window over the main portal illuminated the whole church. Partly because half of it is destroyed, the light came in strongly, and as the sun sank a fierce beam lit up a horrible discoloration on the stone pavement. " That," said our guide with much feeling, " is the burnt blood of the wounded Germans who had sought refuge in the cathedral and who were done to death by their own incendiary shells. That sign we shall keep for ever as a warning to the world of the danger of Hun ferocity."

BEFORE VERDUN

BEFORE VERDUN [1]

THE TRIUMPH OF FRANCE

BEFORE VERDUN, *March* 4.

WHAT is the secret motive underlying the German attempt to break the French line at Verdun, in which the Crown Prince's Army is incurring such appalling losses ? Is it financial, in view of the coming war loan ? Is it dynastic. Or, is it intended to influence doubting neutrals ? From the evidence of German deserters it is known that the attack was originally intended to take place a month or two hence, when the ground was dry. Premature spring caused the Germans to accelerate their plans. There were two final delays owing to bad weather, and then came the colossal onslaught of February 21.

The Germans made a good many of the mistakes we made at Gallipoli. They announced that something large was pending by closing the Swiss frontier. The French, who were not ready, were also warned by their own astute Intelligence Department. Their *avions* were not idle, and, if confirmation were needed, it was given by deserters, who, surmising the horrors that were to come, crept out of the trenches at night, lay down by the edge of the Meuse till the morning, and then gave themselves up, together with information

[1] This telegram (and the others) was, necessarily, written in great haste and with the military censorship in view. It appeared in whole and in part in more than three thousand newspapers in many languages, at a moment when there was grave anxiety as to the fate of Verdun.

that has since proved to be accurate. Things went wrong with the Germans in other ways. A Zeppelin that was to have blown up important railway junctions on the French line of communications was brought down at Révigny, and incidentally the inhabitants of what remains of that much-bombarded town were avenged by the spectacle of the blazing dirigible crashing to the ground and the hoisting with their own petards of 30 Huns therein. It is not necessary to recapitulate that the gigantic effort of February 21 was frustrated by the coolness and tenacity of the French soldiers and the deadly curtain fire of the French gunners.

Though a great deal of calculated nonsense has been sent out in official *communiqués* and dilated upon by dithyrambic Berlin newspaper correspondents as to the taking by storm of the long-dismantled Fort at Douaumont, nothing whatever has been admitted by the Germans as to the appalling price in blood they have paid since February 21 and are still paying. The French losses are, and have been, insignificant. I know the official figure. It has been verified by conversations with members of the British, French, and American Red Cross Societies, who are obviously in a position to know. The wounded who pass through their hands have, in many cases, come straight from where they have seen dead Germans, as has been described by scores of witnesses, lying as lay the Prussian Guard in the first Battle of Ypres. The evidence of one army as to another army's losses needs careful corroboration, and I have that in the evidence of many German prisoners interrogated singly and independently at the French Headquarters.

Beyond this there are the careful conclusions, checked and sifted, of experienced and competent soldiers, who have every reason not to underestimate the remaining strength of the enemy. These conclusions are, roughly, that of the German Corps known to have been engaged the 3rd and 18th Corps

have been entirely used up, or " spent," as the military
phrase goes. The 7th Reserve Corps has lost half,
and the 15th Corps three-quarters, of its available
strengths. According to these authorities, whose
opinion, I repeat, can be taken as erring on the side
of prudence, the German forces had by the evening
of March 3 " used up," in addition to those already
mentioned, a part of the 113th Division, the 5th
Reserve Corps, and the Bavarian Ersatz Division,
without taking into account the losses of other
reinforcements, whose presence on the battlefield
has not yet been definitely ascertained.

More direct, though possibly less reliable, evidence
was secured by questioning closely a number of the
German prisoners. Among them were men from all
parts of the Empire, Alsatians, Pomeranians, Hessians,
Silesians, Prussians, Hanoverians, Bavarians, Würt-
temburgers, and Prussian Poles. All related experiences
identical in substance, though varying in detail.

The case of one man, belonging to the 3rd Battalion
of the 12th Regiment of the 5th Division of the 3rd
Army Corps may be taken as characteristic. On
the morning of February 28 this prisoner reached
the Fort of Douaumont and found there one battalion
of the 24th Regiment, elements of the 64th Regiment
and of the 3rd Battalion of Jäger. The strength
of his company had been, on February 21, 200 rifles
with four officers. On February 22 it had fallen to
70 rifles, with one officer. The other companies
had suffered similar losses. On February 23 the
prisoner's company was reinforced by 45 men, bearing the numbers of the 12th, the 52nd, the 35th,
and the 205th Regiments. These men had been
drawn from various depôts in the interior. The
men of the 12th Regiment believed that five
regiments were in reserve in the woods behind the
3rd Corps, but, as time went on and losses increased
without any sign of the actual presence of these

reserves, doubt spread whether they were really in existence. The prisoner declared that his comrades were no longer capable of fresh effort.

None of the prisoners questioned estimated the losses suffered by their companies at less than one-third of the total effectives. Taking into account all available indications, it may safely be assumed that, during the fighting of the last 13 days, the Germans have lost in killed, wounded, and prisoners at least 100,000 men.

The profits—as the soldier speaks of such matters— being so small, what then are the overwhelming motives that impel the attack on Verdun, and the chicanery of the German *communiqués* ? Is it for any of the reasons I have given above, or is it an effect of economic pressure which leads to the miscalculation that the possible taking over of the French line at Verdun is a means of ending the war ? The Germans are so wont to misread the minds of other nations that they are quite foolish enough to make themselves believe this or any other foolish thing. It cannot be pretended that the attack has in it anything of military necessity. It was urged forward at a time of year when weather conditions might prove, as they have proved, a serious handicap in such matters as the moving of big guns and the essential observation by aeroplanes.

The district of Verdun lies in one of the coldest and also the most misty sectors in the long line between Nieuport and Switzerland. Changes of temperature, too, are somewhat more frequent here than elsewhere ; and so sudden are these changes that not long ago here occurred, on a part of the front, one of nature's furious and romantic reminders of her power to impose her will. The opposing French and German trenches, their parapets hard frozen, are so close that they are actually within hearing of each other. Towards dawn a rapid thaw set in. The parapets melted and subsided, and two long lines of men stood up naked, as it were, before each other, face to face with only two possibilities—wholesale murder on the one side or the other, or a temporary unofficial peace for the making of fresh parapet protections.

The situation was astounding and unique in the history of trench warfare. The French and German officers, without conferring and unwilling to negotiate, turned their backs so that they might not see officially so unwarlike a scene, and the men on each side rebuilt their parapets without the firing of a single shot.

This instance serves to illustrate the precarious weather in which the Germans have undertaken an adventure in the quick success of which the elements play such a part. That the attack would certainly prove more costly to them than to the French the German Staff must have known. That the sufferings of the wounded lying out through the long nights of icy wind in the No-Man's Land between the lines would be great did not probably disturb the Crown Prince. It is one of the most gruesome facts in the history of the War that the French, peering through the moonlight at what they thought to be stealthily crawling Germans, found them to be wounded men frozen to death.

During the war, in France and in Flanders, in camps and in hospitals, I have conversed with at least 100 Germans. Prisoners' talk is always to be accepted with great reserve, but the prisoners of the Verdun campaign have so plainly horror and misery depicted upon their countenances that I need no other evidence as to the tragedy through which they have passed.

The vast battle of Verdun might have been arranged for the benefit of interested spectators, were it not that the whole zone for miles around the great scene is as tightly closed to the outer world as a lodge of Freemasons. Furnished with every possible kind of pass, accompanied by a member of the French Headquarters Staff in a military car driven by a chauffeur whose steel helmet marked him as a soldier, I was nevertheless held up by intractable gendarmes. My colleague (Mr. Wickham Steed [1]) the chief of the foreign department of *The Times*, who assisted me in the many enquiries I was presently allowed to make in and about the battlefield, was detained with me at a point twenty-five miles away from the great scene. Even at that distance the mournful and unceasing reverberation of the guns was insistent, and, as the sentry examined our papers and waited for telephonic instructions, I counted more than 200 of the distant voices of *Kultur*.

As one gets nearer and nearer the great arena on which the whole world's eyes are turned to-day, proofs of French efficiency and French thoroughness are countless. I do not pretend to any military knowledge other than a few scraps gathered in some half-dozen visits to the War, but the abundance of reserve shells for guns, from mighty howitzers to the graceful French mitrailleuse of the aeroplane, of rifle ammunition, of petrol stores, and of motor-wagons of every description, was remarkable. I can truly say that the volume exceeded anything in my previous experience.

As one approaches the battle the volume of sound becomes louder and at times terrific. And it is curious, the mingling of peace with war. The chocolate and the pneumatic tyre advertisements on the village walls, the kilometre stone with its ten kilo-

---

[1] Mr. Steed speaks French, German and Italian as a native, knows other languages sufficiently for intercourse, and does not object to the voyaging vagaries of his friend, the writer of the fragments that make up this book. During our Italian, Swiss, Spanish and French rush in the autumn, in most part of which he was with me, he tells me that our sleep average was three and a half hours in each twenty-four.—N.

metres to Verdun, a village curé peacefully strolling along the village street, just as though it were March, 1914, and his congregation had not been sent away from the war zone, while their houses were filled by a swarming army of men in pale blue. Such a wonderful blue this new French invisible cloth! A squadron of cavalry in the new blue and their steel helmets passes at the moment, and gives the impression that one is back again in what were known as the romantic days of war.

When one has arrived at the battlefield, there are a dozen vantage points from which with glasses, or, indeed, with the naked eye, one can take in much that has happened. Verdun lies in a great basin with the silvery Meuse twining in the valley. The scene is, on the whole, Scottish. Verdun, from where I saw it, might be Perth, and the Meuse the Tay. Small groups of firs darken some of the hills, giving a natural resemblance to Scotland.

The town is being made into a second Ypres by the Germans. Yet, as it stands out in the sunlight, it is difficult to realize that it is a place whose people have all gone, save a few of the faithful who live below ground. (Ypres looked like that the first time I saw it soon after the war began.) The tall towers of Verdun still stand. Close by us is a hidden French battery, and it is pretty to see the promptitude with which it sends its screaming shells back to the Germans within a few seconds of the dispatch of a missive from the Huns. One speedily grows accustomed to the sound and the scene, and can follow the position of the villages about which the Germans endeavour to mislead the world by wireless every morning.

We journey farther afield, and the famous fort of Douaumont is pointed out. The storming of Fort Douaumont as related by the German despatches is on a par with the sinking of the *Tiger* and the recent air bombardment of Liverpool. All the world knows

that the *Tiger* is, as she was before the Germans sank
her in their newspapers, one of the finest ships in the
world, and that the air bombardment of Liverpool
was imagined in Berlin. The storming of Fort
Douaumont, gunless and unmanned, was about as
important, a military operation of little value. A
number of the Brandenburgers climbed into the
gunless fort, and some of them are still there,
supplied precariously with food by their comrades
at night. They are practically surrounded by the
French, whose Headquarters Staff regard the whole
incident as a simple episode in the give-and-take of
war. The announcement of the fall of Fort Douaumont to the world evinces the great anxiety of the
Germans to magnify anything concerning Verdun
into a great event. It should also cause people to
apply a grain of salt to German official *communiqués*
before swallowing them.

These modern battles have now been described so
frequently that there is little new to be written of them.
Of the conflict at Verdun it can be said that on a fine
day and out of sight of the horrors of the hand-to-
hand encounters its surroundings make it a beautiful
battle. There is rather more bird life in this part of
France than in some others, and we noticed with
particular interest the spirit and the cheerful song of a
lark as it climbed skywards hard by the spot where a
French " 75 " was splitting the ears with its snap and
scream.

As we leave the battlefield and come to where is
the first Red Cross Station it rejoices our English eyes
to notice the number of English ambulances bearing
the inscription of the British Red Cross and the Order
of St. John of Jerusalem, which are allowed to aid
the French. It will please the miners and mine-
owners of Derbyshire and Nottinghamshire to know
that many of the wonderful carriages are of their
gift. The Red Cross flags that flutter pathetically

gay, as the cars rush along the well-cared-for road, make one anxious, but a few enquiries prove that the losses of the day have been inconsiderable.

As night falls we come across our first convoy of the great hooded motor lorries, which my companion counted by the thousand while we were on our way between Paris and the Meuse. The War has reduced motor transport to a science, and in no way is French efficiency better demonstrated than in the manner in which they have added to the carrying capacity of their railways and great canals. They have utilized thousands of miles of poplar and lime-lined roads for mechanical transport at 15 miles an hour. On one road alone we counted 20 motor convoys, each composed of about a hundred wagons, and each group indicated by some simple mark, such as a four-leaved shamrock, an ace of hearts, or a comet.

Who are the men who are organizing the great battle for the French side ? Let me at once say that they are young men. General Pétain, one of the discoveries of the war, till lately colonel, is still in his late fifties ; most of the members of his staff are much younger. One hears of luxury at Headquarters, but I have not experienced it, either at our own Headquarters or at the French. General Pétain, when I enjoyed his hospitality at luncheon, drank tea. Most of his young men contented themselves with water, or the white wine of the Meuse.

In the brief meal he allowed himself the General discussed the battle as though he were merely an interested spectator. In appearance he resembles Lord Roberts, though he is of larger build. In accordance with the drastic changes that the French, like the Germans, are making in their Command, his rise has been so rapid that he is little known to the French people, though greatly trusted by General Joffre and the Government. I naturally did not ask his opinion on any matters connected

M

with the War. We discussed the Australians, the Canadians, the great growth of the British Army, and kindred matters.

At another gathering of officers someone asked whether the French would not expect the British to draw off the Germans by making an attack in the West. " It is questionable," replied one young officer, " whether such an attack would not involve disproportionate losses that would weaken the Allies." The same officer pointed out that, although the capture of Verdun would cause great regret, owing to the historic name it bears, it would not, for many reasons, be more important than the pressing back of any other similar number of miles on the front. Forts being of little account since the introduction of the big German hammers, he believed that General Sarrail had said that the question was not one merely of dismantling the forts, but of blowing them up. As it is, whenever the Germans capture a piece of land where an old fort happens to be, they will use it as an advertisement. But though the French officers are not looking to us, so far as I could learn, for active co-operation *now*, they are most certainly urging that when our new armies and their officers are trained we shall aid them by bearing our full share of the tremendous military burden they are carrying.

The present attack on the French at Verdun is by far the most violent incident of the whole Western War. As I write it is late. Yet the bombardment is continuing, and the massed guns of the Germans are of greater calibre than has ever been used in such numbers. The superb calm of the French people, the efficiency of their organization, the equipment of their cheery soldiery, convince one that the men in the German machine would never be able to compare with them even if France had not the help of Russia, the five British nations, Belgium, Serbia,

Italy, and Japan. It is unsafe to prophesy about war, as it is to prophesy about any other human affair, but this prediction one can make, and with certainty : that, whatever may be the result of the attack on the Verdun sector, every such effort will result in adding many more thousands of corpses to those now lying in the valley of the Meuse, the numbers of which are being so carefully concealed from the neutral world and the Germans themselves ; and could neutrals see the kind of men whom the Germans do not scruple to use as soldiers their faith in Teutonic physical efficiency would receive a shock.

Unluckily a pygmy behind a machine-gun is the equal of a giant. " What a pity your Highlanders cannot meet these fellows in fair fight," said a French officer, as we reviewed a gang of prisoners. " The war would be over in a month." Personal contact with the miserable creatures who form the bulk of the German prisoners here is needed to convince an observer that such specimens of humanity can really have belonged to the German Army, and especially to a *corps d'élite* such as the 3rd, or Berlin, Army Corps. One ill-favoured youth hailing from Charlottenburg was barely 5ft. 4in. high. Narrow-chested and peak-faced, he had the quick-wittedness of the urban recruit, but seemed far better fitted for his stool as a railway clerk than for the life of the trenches or for the ordeal of attack. Yet he had been taken at the end of 1914 and sent to Flanders after six weeks' training, " educated " in trench-making for another month, than left to fend for himself and his comrades as a full-fledged Prussian eaglet. Like the bulk of the other prisoners belonging to other units, he had been withdrawn at the beginning of February from the Flanders front and sent to the neighbourhood of Verdun. He had known that there was to be an attack, but until the order was actually given neither he nor his comrades had received any hint of the precise purpose of the operation in which he was to be employed.

Of one thing he and his fellows were heartily glad— to be taken away from the neighbourhood of the "frightful" English and nearer to the kindly French. From all the reports which these men had received from their families during the last two months it appears that, in the words of one of them, "there reigns in Germany considerable misery." All agreed that butter is unobtainable, meat scarce (except in Alsace and parts of Pomerania), fat almost unknown. In most respects the food of the Army was tolerable, though not good or abundant. All declared that enthusiasm for the war had long since evaporated, though, as two of the more intelligent among them maintained, the German Army does not expect to be beaten, even if it no longer hopes to win. The chief longing of these men, as of their families, was for peace.

The only good thing about these prisoners was their foot-gear. Their stout Blücher boots were an object-lesson in the necessity of tightening certain features of our blockade and of adding a shortage of leather to the other deficiencies of the military and civil supply that are wearing down the German power of resistance.

The true moral of the fighting to the north and east of Verdun is that the French, with a comparatively small loss of ground, have warded off the attack of armies outnumbering them originally by three to one. The German order of battle on February 21 running eastwards from a point north of Varennes comprised on the extreme German right the 7th Reserve Corps, consisting of the 2nd Landwehr Division, the 11th Reserve Division, and the 12th Reserve Division in the order named. During the fighting the 11th Reserve Division is understood to have been relieved by the 22nd Reserve Division.

Immediately before the French line to the north-east of Verdun lay the 14th Reserve Division, with the 7th Reserve Corps and the 11th Bavarian Reserve Division in support.   These troops were on the right of what may be called the central force.   Next to them was ranged the 18th Corps, the 3rd Corps, the 15th Corps, and the Bavarian Ersatz Division in the order named, while south of Etain in the Woevre were ranged the 5th Landwehr Division, the 5th Army Corps, and the 3rd Bavarian Corps opposite Fresnes.

By March 3 the Germans brought up the 113th Reserve Division in place of the spent units of the 3rd Army Corps, while the forces farther to the east and south were relieved or replaced by other units whose composition is not yet exactly known.

There are no means of estimating how long the battle of Verdun may still rage.   To say that the French are confident of holding their own is not enough.   They feel that they have the measure of the enemy, both in men and *matériel*.   They know that, given the necessary concentration of heavy artillery, either side can drive the other from the first, or even from the second, positions, but that, unless the bombardment be followed up by infantry attacks of far greater vigour and persistence than any yet executed by the enemy, and unless the advance of the enemy's artillery can keep pace with that of the infantry, the defending force will have time to make its third position practically impregnable.

This is what has happened round Verdun.   To the north and the north-east the first and second French lines were obliterated by an intense bombardment executed with guns of which the smallest were 105 mm., while the bulk were 210 mm.   Large numbers of still heavier weapons up to 380 mm. were freely used both in direct and in curtain fire.   The weakness of the French forces holding the first and second lines accounts for the insignificance of the losses.   Ground

having thus been gained by the Germans to the north
the French evacuated voluntarily the marshy ground
east of the Verdun Ridges in the Woevre.

The effect of this action was threefold.   It gave the
French a strong defensive line on high ground, it
prevented the formation of a dangerous salient, and,
apparently, it induced the Germans to believe that
their enemy was demoralized.

Verdun is unlikely to be taken.   Nothing justifies
a belief that the spirit and the stamina of the German
forces are equal to the task of dislodging the French
from their present formidable positions.

THE NEW LITTLE BELGIAN ARMY

THE NEW LITTLE BELGIAN ARMY

HEADQUARTERS OF THE BELGIAN ARMY,
Friday, March 17, 1916.

THE little army that first arrested the rush of the Huns, the army that gave the Allies invaluable breathing time, has been fighting longer than any of us.

And it is not too much to say that the world's debt to Belgium has increased steadily since those hectic hours at Liége and Antwerp. The United States recognizes its share in the work for civilization by helping to feed the six millions of Belgians who are holding themselves so proudly while under the immediate domination of the tyrant.

I had been with the Belgian Army soon after its long series of rearguard actions. It was then suffering from its great losses ; it was war weary, and it needed sleep and equipment. It had never lost heart or discipline.

To-day it is the same army, but renewed. It has no great reserves to fall back upon, because the greater part of the nation is imprisoned. The wise men who administer it under the affectionate care of the King have, therefore, while getting into the ranks every possible available Belgian of military age, wherever he may be, devoted themselves to the work of refitting and reorganizing. The result is a perfect little army.

Belgium is above all things fortunate in having

a man. For beyond question one of the most vital of all the forces among the Allies is the Belgian Minister of War, Baron de Broqueville. For years before the outbreak of hostilities *The Times* had consistently called attention to de Broqueville's work and warnings. Except for those warnings Belgium would not have been in a position to offer the resistance it did to the Monster. De Broqueville is fifty-three and looks younger—though I notice the war has not left him unmarked since our last meeting. He is as alive as our Mr. Hughes, and it is remarkable that the views of the two men are alike.

When I arrived at the house, within hearing of the guns, in which he spends alternate weeks between his visits to Havre, his secretary, the young Comte de Lichtervelde, had just finished reading to him one of Mr. Hughes's speeches. Monsieur de Lichtervelde, who knows England and the United States very well indeed, makes it his duty, as part of his secretarial work, to keep his chief well informed in world happenings. A courier each afternoon brings that same morning's *Times*.

M. de Broqueville, who is as good-looking and well-groomed as he is alert, discussed the whole of the European and world situation incisively, frankly, and with a vigour and directness most refreshing to one whose misfortune it is to dwell within reach of the miasmic exhalations of the Upas Tree of Westminster. Some of our Germano-phils twit Mr. Hughes with not being an expert on Germany. That charge cannot be brought against M. de Broqueville, whose country knows, alas! too much of peaceful penetration by commerce, capture of public opinion by subsidization, and political, educational, artistic, and musical espionage. And so Mr. Hughes from Australia and the Baron de Broqueville from Brussels agree exactly as to the Huns. Like all Belgians of the ruling class, de Broqueville is deeply grateful for British help, and is a warm admirer of the steady improvement in our Army. But I had not come to —— to discuss politics or to receive compliments. My desire was to revisit the soldiers with whom I had sojourned after their bloodily-contested retreat against overwhelming forces.

So, after gaining a great deal of extremely interesting information which I do not propose to present to the Germans, and enquiring after Mme. de Broqueville, who has remained courageously at Brussels while her husband takes charge of his King's Government, I made my way by road to the enchanting little sixteenth-century scene where the brain of the Belgian Army is installed.

Army headquarters are very much the same everywhere, save as to their situation. General Wielemans, who is Chief of Staff of his Majesty the King, the Commander-in-Chief, has very capable advisers in General Biebuyck, Aide-de-Camp to the King, and General D'Orjo, M. de Broqueville's Chef de Cabinet. General Wielemans, who speaks English and knows England well, asked me what I should particularly like to see, and arranged that the next day I should be taken along the Belgian trenches by Colonel Detail, under Chief of Staff.

Though the shortest of the lines held by the Allies, the Belgian line is, in proportion to the free Belgian population, much the longest. It occupies a difficult and extremely uncomfortable position, for in no part of the war zone is the mud of Flanders blacker and deeper than in the Belgian trenches.

I told General Wielemans that what the English public would be interested to learn something about is the very efficient Belgian artillery which has rendered so excellent an account of itself. It is no secret that Belgian preparations were not such as Baron de Broqueville had for years urged, but in the matter of artillery the gallant little army had acquired great proficiency, doubtless partly by reason of its association with those masters of the gun, the French. That the Belgians are well equipped with great cannon, big howitzers, 75's, and machine-guns, and that every gun has a plentiful supply of shells of every description is abundantly well known to Hans and Fritz on the other side of the inundations and elsewhere along the Belgian front.

I asked General Wielemans if he would allow me to take a quiet and unobtrusive seat in one of his batteries during such time as an artillery duel was timed to rage vigorously. He readily assented, and I was taken by M. de Lichtervelde and Colonel Detail to Lieutenant General de Ceunink, who, with Major-General Orth, after some consultation, found me at a considerable distance a particularly lively young artillery officer, whose four " pets," as he called them in English, were timed to perform that afternoon.

Our way lay through ruined sixteenth-century Flemish villages, where the churches in almost every case had been shelled to fragments and where also in almost every case the carved wooden Christ (often as not of the fervent Spanish type dating from Spanish times) remained, as by some miracle, untouched.

I was long loth to believe that the Germans selected churches as artillery objectives, but personal examination of more that 100 shelled towns proves it. And with the churches usually goes the churchyard; open coffins, shrouded corpses, and grinning skulls show that the modern Prussian takes as much pleasure in revealing the secrets of the grave as he does in the destruction of his enemy's wife and child.

In one of the small ruined towns we visited, three hundred of the population still remained, and will not leave. An old, old man was bending over a little garden, a lusty young woman was scrubbing at a tub while her little son was playing with shell fragments. The whole district, every street and open place, was a series of gigantic *trous de marmites* (shell holes), filled with water, in one of which a couple of little people were sailing a paper boat. There were no guns or anything military whatever in the town, but it was being bombarded periodically by Germans, probably in reply to dexterous British artillery work at Ypres.

It is a thousand pities that expert kinematograph operators are not sent to these places to prove to the world that German warfare, especially in these later days of the conflict, is at least as much directed against the civil population as against the military. French gunners score a success in Champagne, and, in reply, the Germans throw asphyxiating shells into Reims, and so on in all the theatres of war.

I do not propose to give the least indication of the situation of the battery with which I spent some very interesting hours. The Huns have never found it, nor, indeed, any of the French or Belgian batteries I have entered. For the detective powers of the aeroplane observer have been countered by extraordinary ingenuity in concealment on the part of artillerymen.

There was the usual dog attached to it, some sort of mongrel that always seems to like to be with men in dangerous places. By an ingenious arrangement of barbed wire a nice large cage of starlings, finches, and sparrows, who did not in the least mind the guns, had been arranged ; they were hopping merrily and eating well. A spring garden with crocuses and primroses had been planted.

The dug-outs had all sorts of amusing names ; one was called " The Virtuous Repose," and another, in English, " Home, Sweet Home." The captain in charge of the battery, who had been alongside

and among the English in the early stages of the war
and had picked up a good deal of English, which,
like most Belgians, he liked to exercise, speedily
explained the system on which he worked his 75's,
for each of which he had a pet name. He showed
me his map, with frequent aeroplane corrections in
red ink, of the enemy's position in front of him.
He demonstrated the extreme facility of the elevating
and deflecting apparatus of his four favourites.
He had not yet received his instructions as to what
was to be the programme of his day's work. They
would come by telephone from certain Headquarters.
Meanwhile, I might like to go down into his " wine
cellar " and see the excellent array of " bottles,"
as he called them.

We bent low and went deep, deep into the earth,
and his electric torch revealed a fine display of
shells. Some had been made in England. There
were several types of shells and several kinds of
fuzes. " Very good bottles indeed, *hein ?* " he said
in broken English.

We came above ground again and listened to
the various forms of artillery that were to be heard
around us. " Those," he said, asking me to listen
to a continuous series of salvoes, " are your English-
men. Plenty shells now." Miles away there was
the deep roar of something big, reminding me of
the voices of Verdun. " That," he remarked, " is
Belgian howitzer." The men were smoking and
waiting about, taking no notice whatever of the
occasional burstings of German messages that threw
up great clouds of mud.

Suddenly there came the ring of the telephone
bell, taking one for the moment quickly back to
London, but carrying a very different message from
that which one receives in one's office.

Instantaneously the men sprang down to their
guns, and then I saw the marvellous working of

these 75's, whose sharp bang, bang I have heard at so many points at the front. A quick order was shouted as to the direction and elevation, there was a slight pause, the little chamber and its Rembrandt-like faces were lit up for a moment as by the flame of a smithy, a roar came that was gentle after the earth-shaking at Verdun, and then silence till, kilometres away, we heard our shells bursting.

The gunners were waiting to hear the telephone report from the observer. Within a few seconds it was received—" Too short."

Another try. " Too far " came the verdict.

At the third shot came the report, " A hit," and then was revealed to me the magic of the 75.

The gun recoils so quickly that it can be stoked with shells and fired, in the hands of really trained gunners, with a speed most extraordinary to watch.

I remember well the first time that I saw a cannon fired in war. I did so with reluctance, not wishing to participate even by observation in the sending forth of that which would destroy life, or wound. But the spectacle of these smashed towns and babies' graves in France and Belgium has removed any sentimental nonsense of that kind from my conception of war, and so, knowing that these Belgian gunners were helping to weary and destroy the *moral* of an army that did not disdain to initiate gas poisoning and the throwing of flame and even vitriol, I confess to enthusiastic rejoicing at this remarkable little organization that is only one of hundreds the Belgians possess.

A good artillery battle reminds one very much of a quick lawn-tennis volley, and in this matter of artillery reply the Latins certainly are speedier than the Huns.

A signal presently brought the order to cease fire from this particular battery, and immediately afterwards a little further down the line other voices spoke.

We made our way back through the mud to a distant highway, and then a long walk brought us to our motor, which was sheltered behind one of the few walls still remaining in that district.

At a very pleasant and simple Headquarters repast, Verdun, the English Fleet, and the latest wireless were discussed, and then everyone went about his business. Army Headquarters have settled down to the regulation and prompt routine of all efficient business organizations. The improved Belgian Army, as regards the higher command, efficiency, equipment, cavalry, infantry, artillery, and transport is, like our own, the creation of nearly nineteen months of war, and it is said that war is the best school for war.

Nor are the medical arrangements of the Army neglected. Inspector-General Melis, who is well known in England, and is a hard-headed, practical man, had to deal with almost insuperable difficulties when the Germans seized practically the whole of the Belgian Red Cross *matériel* in their advance. He has excellent hospitals at various points that need not be mentioned, lest they tempt Hun gunners unduly. There is one little English hospital which I must not forget—the Belgian Field Hospital. Its windows rattle night and day with the vibration of the guns. Its career has been one of adventure, for it began life at Antwerp in September, 1914.

On the night I paid my respects the Belgian Field Hospital was quite full. I found an excellent Scotch doctor and matron, and a number of devoted nurses, who have been with it since the day it started travelling across Belgium, during the time it was shelled out of Furnes, where I had seen it before, and throughout all its vicissitudes. The whole establishment is ready, if necessary, at any moment to move again.

Among the patients that day were a number who were desperately wounded by a very common form of accident. Souvenir rings from the trenches are being sought for all over the world. They are made of aluminium obtained from the German fuzes, and unexploded fuzes are the cause of numerous fatalities.

In every ward of this hospital, in every Belgian dug-out, in every room I entered in the little part of Belgium that is now in Belgian hands, and on the table of the Minister of War and his General, are pictures of the heroic King and Queen, who are known by sight to every soldier in the army, and to whom the whole of this very efficient Belgian force is deeply devoted.

WITH THE ITALIANS

WITH THE ITALIANS

SOME TELEGRAMS FROM THE VARIOUS FRONTS

HEARING that an Italian offensive was about to commence, and having an invitation from His Majesty the King of Italy, the Italian Commander-in-Chief, and also from General Cadorna, his Chief of Staff, I hastened from the Battle of the Somme to the Italian Headquarters at Udine, and was able to arrive in time for the capture of the important keystone town of Gorizia.

I spent some time with the Italian Army, and dispatched telegrams almost daily to my newspapers, some of which are reproduced in this volume.

I

IN GORIZIA

GORIZIA, *August* 10.

To have broken bread well inside enemy territory is quite a new experience in the War.

This afternoon I had an excellent Austrian meal at the Grosses Café in Gorizia. As recently as Tuesday this despatch would have been dated Gorizia, Austria. To-day, though pink and white Austrian shrapnel is still bursting fitfully over the town, Gorizia is firmly Italian. The hoardings are covered with German advertisements, German newspapers still hang in the

racks outside the shops, but the brilliant green, white,
and red Italian flag with the Cross of Savoy flutters
from the windows of many of the beautiful villas
along the Corso Francesco Giuseppe. The inhabitants
wish that the shelling would cease, but the pro-
Italians wave friendly signals to the serried masses
of grey-clad infantry with blue steel helmets who are
sweeping through the delightful city on their way to
the conquest of the Carso.

It will please believers in the mounted arm to know
that cavalry are already taking part in the pursuit,
and are expectant of great things in the near future.
With the cavalry is the cavalry on wheels—grey
armoured motor-cars—which the Austrians after their
bitter experience of the last few days are known to
dread.

We entered what was till lately Austrian territory
at Cormons ; and, after pushing our way for an hour
and a half through clouds of dust raised by the out-
going transport of men, great guns, ammunition, and
food, and the incoming motors of the Croce Rossa
Italiana and the British Red Cross, we arrived in
sight of the serpentine Isonzo, the bluest of rivers.
Here we left our car in hiding and walked, sometimes
under cover, and sometimes in the open to the lower
bridge which the Italian engineers with wonderful
promptness have already repaired. On our way we
examined the Italian and Austrian trenches, which for
many long months had been within speaking distance
of each other. So accurate was the Italian artillery
fire that, while their own trenches—neatly lined with
steel lattice work new to me—were intact, those of
the enemy—which appear to be lined with a kind of
basket work, such as is often seen in Tirol—were
almost as badly smashed as the German trenches on
the Somme.

On our left rose Monte Sabotino, the key to the
whole formidable bridgehead of Gorizia. When on

Sunday last it was taken by the Italians, its loss, combined with the terrific bombardment that has so sadly marred the charm of Gorizia, caused the Austrians to flee.

There is a joyousness in accompanying a triumphant army in its progress, and a strange sense of pleasure in being in the enemy's own city, which he thought impregnable. Even in this part of Austria Hun *Kultur* has left its familiar mark on architectural style, a mark as familiar as his advertisements, familiar as his beer—indeed, a soldier-waiter at the *café* suggested waggishly that the suddenness of the Austrian retreat was due to a scarcity of beer occasioned by the hot weather. How unexpected was the retreat may be gathered from the fact that among the booty were many mules laden with hot rolls for the " high-well-born " breakfast of the Austrian Hauptquartier.

The good folk of Gorizia were plucking up courage to come out of the cellars [1] as we made our way to present our respects to the General Commanding the victorious troops. The remarkable strategy by which General Cadorna deluded the Austrians and their German masters into believing that he was about to attack in the Trentino some hundreds of miles to the west is probably now well known in England, and how he moved night after night several army corps to the appointed spot, getting the last battery into position half an hour before the moment fixed for the opening bombardment.

No better General for the final blow on Gorizia could have been selected by General Cadorna. I offered him congratulations in the name of the Allies and of *The Times*, and though worn out by continuous fighting since Sunday last, and unshaven and without sleep, he was prompt and alert. He said :—" I hope

[1] There were Italians among them who had lain concealed for months with yard-long beards and hair.

to do better.   Our front line is now several miles
beyond Gorizia, and the cavalry is getting to work."
I asked him whether the enemy had another strong
line this side of Trieste ; and, though his military
prudence precluded a positive reply, his gestures
revealed hopefulness.

This General's fighting record dates from the war
of 1870, when, 18 years of age, he volunteered to
fight for France under Bourbaki, and was promoted
officer for valour in the field.   At the age of 20 he
entered the military service of his own country.   His
political services have been not less distinguished.
For some time he belonged to the Italian Parliament,
urging in season and out of season the need for military reform.

As we prepared to leave this very handsome tree-
embowered city, for the capture of which all Italy is
now beflagged, we were detained some time by acute
shelling of the Isonzo bridge—the last desperate
attention of the retreating Austrians.   It was gratify-
ing to notice that among the first visitors to Gorizia
was Mr. George Macaulay Trevelyan, in charge of the
British Red Cross Service.   His chief anxiety was to
ascertain whether he would be able to get the British
ambulances across the damaged Isonzo bridge.

II

HOW GORIZIA WAS TAKEN

ITALIAN HEADQUARTERS, *August* 11

THE more the Italian offensive on the Isonzo is studied, the greater does its significance appear, and the clearer is manifest the ability of the strategic conception on which it was based.

Every great commander takes account of the mental disposition of the enemy. General Cadorna carefully traded upon the Austrian belief that the Italian efforts would be concentrated upon the Trentino front, and neglected no means of humouring the enemy's fancy. The Austrians also imagined that if any action were undertaken on the Isonzo it would be nearer the sea—from Monfalcone. In this respect also General Cadorna humoured them. Then, when the hour struck for the offensive against the Gorizia bridgehead, the enemy found that Italian artillery in overwhelming strength and masses of men had been swiftly transferred from the Trentino by road and rail ready to wrest from the Hapsburg forces the positions on which they had worked for as many years as the Germans on the Somme had worked for months.

The credit for the brilliant conception naturally belongs to General Cadorna, but the glory of the achievement falls to the Duke of Aosta's Third Army. Quivering with impatience as the bombardment reduced the enemy observation posts and rocky redoubts on Monte Sabotino the Duke of Aosta's soldiers swarmed from the saps secretly driven through the rock up to within a few yards of the Austrian lines and overwhelmed the foe in a mad, victorious rush. In a few hours Sabotino Hill, the key to Gorizia and the bridgehead, and the scene of the hardest and bloodiest fighting on this part of the front since the war began, was firmly in Italian hands.

Across the Isonzo and further south the long ridge and summits of San Michele were simultaneously carried. Details of the fighting in this sector of the battlefield are still lacking, but the rapidity of the progress may be judged from the reported occupation of Doberdo yesterday.

Nevertheless the stout Austrian resistance on Hill 240, the highest summit of the Podgora ridge on the west bank of the river, delayed for some hours the actual assault on Gorizia. The enemy already knew that Gorizia was doomed. During the night from Monday to Tuesday orders were given for the evacuation of the city, though the massive stone viaduct that spans the Isonzo just north of the iron bridge we crossed on Thursday was only blown up at 5.30 on Tuesday morning.

The resistance of Hill 240 being at length overcome, the Italian infantry, debouching from Podgora, swarmed forward to the river with inimitable dash. With water up to their necks, carrying their rifles above their heads and shouting patriotic songs, they forded the broad stream and carried the eastern bank. The enemy shrapnel, which churned the water into foam, failed to check their progress. Men wounded in the water insisted on being helped to gain the eastern bank, saying, " Then they'll not send us back."

By this time the bulk of the Austrian forces were in full retreat, but the rearguard offered a stiff resistance. The Italian guns skilfully covered the advance, sweeping the approaches to the city and keeping down the enemy fire. The most pleasant surprise for the Italians was the comparative feebleness of the Austrian fire from Monte Santo, some distance north-east. Indeed, the question constantly arose, Where were the Austrian guns ? Had they been hurriedly removed or knocked out by the Italian bombardment— or sent to Galicia or the Trentino ? Be the explanation what it may, the fact remains that the unexpectedness of the Italian offensive took the Austrians at great disadvantage in regard to artillery, as in other respects. Had Monte Santo been heavily held with big guns the Italian crossing of the Isonzo and the occupation of Gorizia would have been far more difficult and costly than they actually were.

Meanwhile the Italian batteries deluged Gorizia with shrapnel. Some hundreds of civilians inevitably suffered from the iron hail, while the walls of many villas along the spacious Corso Francesco Giuseppe are severely pock-marked. The pavements are littered with broken glass and tiles. The advancing Italian troops found hot work in clearing the outskirts and some houses, but as soon as the task was accomplished they swept on, and the tricolour was run up on the principal buildings. Then masses of troops pushed over the Isonzo iron bridge, which the engineers smartly repaired under heavy fire. Battery after battery of field artillery galloped across, some losing a few horses on the way, but none faltering. Cyclists, Carabinieri, and cavalry followed rapidly.

When I visited Gorizia yesterday the streets were full of cavalry. I should not be surprised to hear that before nightfall on Thursday a strong cavalry cordon had been thrown around the whole region from Gorizia southwards to Doberdo and Monfalcone.

The Austrian positions on the western bank of the Isonzo presented many points of exceptional strength. Under the embankment which carries the road to the iron bridge runs a long stone-lined tunnel connected on both sides with deep communication trenches. In this tunnel 600 Austrians were caught as they were waiting with machine-guns to take the advancing Italians in the rear.

The railway arch on the other side was also strongly held. Rents and gashes in its corrugated iron roof bear witness to the accuracy of the Italian fire, while twisted iron girders and the railings of the iron bridge over the river prove that here the Austrian big guns had the range to a nicety.

The road and the battlefield on either side of the river are littered with traces of the struggle. Austrian and Italian entrenching tools, leather cartridge pouches, hand grenades, aerial torpedoes, trench mortars, broken rifles, knapsacks, and rolled blankets litter the ground.

In the heat and dust of an Italian August day the weight of the accoutrements which the Italian infantryman carries into battle is apt to become intolerable. When one has trudged, lightly clad, a few miles along roads ankle-deep in fine dust under the afternoon sun one understands the puissant charm of the neat water-tank carts that are never far in the rear of the Italian advance.

III

THE CARSO BATTLES

A Thirsty Desert

Isonzo Front, *August* 13.

Of the ferocious fighting on the Italian front little is understood in England. If the figures of the wounded carried by the British Red Cross ambulances alone could be published, they would, perhaps, open the eyes of the public. Let me select one battle scene, one in which the crumbling of Austria is visible even without field-glasses—on the birdless, waterless Carso. It is certainly the thirstiest battlefield this side of Suez. It can only be compared to a gigantic Shap fell or Devonshire tor. It is not unlike the Arizona desert without the alkali.

As another battlefield, look at the Calvaria position, on the Podgora hill outside Gorizia on the west bank of the Isonzo river. Take the steepest wooded hillside you know ; put the Austrians, deeply and cunningly entrenched, on the top ; and realize that the capture of that one hill has cost Italy 15 months' bloodshed. The price was great, though the thousand deeds of herosim which resulted in the sudden flight of the Austrians should thrill generations of Italians yet unborn.

These are but two of the battlefields of Italy which are barely known to the outside world. They deserve to be known.

These sturdy Piedmontese, Lombards, Sicilians, Neapolitans, have all fought with equal valour.

Owing to the preoccupation of the world with the rest of the war and the absence of newspaper correspondents, the impression of the Italian forces received throughout the world has been that of a *dilettante* army. For the same reasons that at first made the progress of the British Army slow, Italy is only now beginning to put forth something like her real strength. She has much strength in reserve. A most distinguished Italian officer remarked :—" What we have done now has been good, useful work which we could have done a year ago had we had guns and ammunition."

Yet there should be no mistake about the strength of the Austrian defensive organizations. They are not of the same nature as those of the Germans, because the *terrain* here is entirely different. For example, to make an impression on the rocky soil of the Carso pneumatic drills and dynamite were essential. The Austrian front line has been blasted and drilled out of the limestone rock with machinery similar to that used in making the St. Gothard and Simplon tunnels. The snipers' lookouts are armoured with iron plates an inch thick cemented into the rock. The making of dug-outs must have required the labour by night and day with drill and dynamite of hordes of Croats, Magyars, Slovaks, Swabians, Rumanes, and other races of the Austro-Hungarian Monarchy.

I went out to see 13,000 of these stout fellows just captured in this offensive. They reminded me exactly of the raw, lusty labourers who used to land from emigrant ships at Quebec before the war and were drafted out to make the great transcontinental railways of Canada. Many of them have spent some time in American railroad building and speak English. Their officers are very good imitations of the closely-shorn, square-headed, heel-clicking Prussians in long grey cloaks. Though not Prussians they fight well.

The Austrians have had unlimited ammunition, tons of which have been left behind on the battle-fields. On the Carso their lines had been supplied with water pumped up from various points by oil engines. Food has been abundant—four square meals daily. They look shabby—all prisoners look shabby —but they have invariably excellent boots, characteristic of the Hun and his dupes.

Viewed from the mountain vantage points the 30-mile battle is a beautiful and grandiose scene. The battle line now runs far beyond Gorizia—a town resembling Homburg or Baden Baden—which, when you get into it, is seen to be dominated by a fine *Schloss* fitfully shelled by the retreating Austrians with pink and white shrapnel. On the hillsides great shells are bursting and here and there a burning copse or village sends a tall column of smoke into the limpid air. The sound of guns firing from concealed positions reverberates from hill to hill on either side of the Isonzo valley, while great shells which the Italian soldiers call "tramcars" whiz through the sunshine like enormous invisible rockets.

The whole line of battle is visibly moving forwards. The Italian projectiles hourly burst a little farther eastwards. The enemy is not running, but is clearly retreating. The capture of Oppacchiasella and Hill 121 on the Carso tells its own tale, and, though strong positions like Monte Santo and San Gabriele still resist to the northward, the Italian advance is steady. Steady also is the inflow of prisoners. Two thousand more were brought in yesterday. Where will the retreat end? Opinions differ, but the matter is emphatically not one for public discussion.

" It is difficult for me to express my feelings about what we have seen to-day," said a distinguished young officer who accompanied us and who was the first to enter Oppacchiasella on Friday. " Italy needs the self-confidence that comes of military achievement. Now she has it. It will broaden her shoulders and steady her national life in every way. When I think of the transformation these months of war have wrought in me, who am 30, how much greater must it be in all our young soldiers of 19 and 20 ! "

Italy has, indeed, done herself credit—that is, justice. I have described the Austrian defences. The Italian are no less perfect. Line after line of strongly built works, league upon league of splendid roads, motor transport service, food and water supply, all reveal her powers of organization.

We toiled yesterday under a burning sun along miles of the rugged Carso—the harsh German name "Karst" seems apter for this inhospitable, rock-strewn plateau, where lizards alone find life bearable—past where last week had been the Italian and Austrian first line positions. In one night the Italian engineers had hammered and hewn across the bare limestone a tolerable road which to-morrow will be smooth enough for motor vehicles. Warm food—the excellent Italian *minestrone*, a thick soup composed of meat, vegetables, rice, and macaroni—was being brought up on mule back to the danger zone and carried thence by hand to the firing line.

One gruesome sight in the former No Man's Land between the first positions bore witness to the character of the climate. We came upon the remains of a human body in a kneeling posture absolutely mummified by the scorching heat amid the brambles, thistles, wild roses, and scraggy mountain ash, which form the only vegetation in this desolate region. While collecting battle souvenirs for a boy friend at home I discovered that, during the hot hours of the day, metal objects can only be handled with difficulty.

A strange feature of the Carso are the deep, crater-like depressions called *doline*, filled with dark brown,

peaty earth, every one of which forms a natural fort.
The Austrian troops fortify them and build officers'
shelters in their sides. One such group of shelters
had been devastated by the Italian bombardment.
The occupants had fled, abandoning vast quantities
of ammunition, entrenching tools, whole cases marked
" explosive cartridges," piles of rockets, a rich
assortment of hand-grenades, lengths of water hose,
rolls of wire, and other paraphernalia of this uncanny
war. A pestilential odour proved that not all the
inhabitants of these barbaric excavations had fled.
Letters and relics also showed that ladies from Buda-
pest had been not infrequent visitors.

In nothing is the disorganization of the Austrian
defence more clearly revealed than in the utter
absence of aerial observation. During my whole
visit to this front I have not seen an Austrian aeroplane
or observation balloon. The Italian captive balloons
float serenely in the still air, directing the fire of their
own batteries, but the Austrians appear to be firing
blindly. The Italian heavy batteries are consequently
able to do their deadly work undisturbed. Their
shells search position after position, bursting with
marvellous accuracy on selected points miles ahead,
and crowning every ridge with dark clouds of smoke.

The enemy's bitterness of soul may be judged by
his behaviour. At Doberdo Russian prisoners of
war, who had been brought like so many of their
comrades to make roads for the Austrians, were
found hanged—possibly as revenge for the escape of
other Russian prisoners who pluckily swam the
Isonzo the other day and reached the Italian lines
after hiding for four nights among the rocks. Italian
wounded were found mutilated. I have seen the
terrible spiked maces habitually used by the Austrians
to break the skulls of the wounded. Equally bar-
barous are the thongs with leaden balls attached to
sticks, which the Austrians use to coerce laggards.

A specimen of these thongs found on Friday was shown to me by an Italian commander of high rank.

The Austrians are inspired by fierce hatred of the Italians, and their brutal conduct may well engender the fury of Italian comrades of victims of such ferocity. But it is very difficult to arouse lasting resentment in the Italian *soldatini*. " You're a filthy dog," said one of them yesterday to a thirsty prisoner. " Here, have a pull at my water-bottle."

Owing to the fact that so many Italian and Austrian soldiers have worked in the United States and Canada, it often happens that English is the only language in which they can mutually converse. Yesterday I saw a small band of prisoners being brought in by Bersaglieri, who answered my remarks upon the stout physical appearance of the prisoners by saying in good New York dialect, " They can holler all right, Mister," at which the prisoners grinned with evident understanding.

On finding, through prisoners, that the news of the Franco-British successes on the Somme and the sweeping Russian advance had been kept from the Austrian rank and file, and that newspapers had long been withheld from the men in the Austrian trenches, General Cadorna, with his customary shrewd alertness, had millions of little news sheets dropped from aeroplanes among the enemy. The news sheets are printed in all the principal languages of the Hapsburg Monarchy. On the other hand, General Cadorna causes all good Italian or Allied news to be telephoned along the whole Italian front line, and, following the German example, he encourages the circulation of newspapers among the troops.

Unfortunately the Italian public, while understanding the immense value of our Fleet, has no idea of the superb British military organization or of the vast assemblage of British and Dominion troops in France. I am repeatedly asked if we have yet 500,000 men in

France, and while great publicity is given to France
and Russia, I find the impression general among
educated classes here that our part in the war is
considered to be progressing unduly slowly, owing
to inadequate supply of trained officers. Beyond Sir
Douglas Haig's official *communiqués* and occasional
second-hand accounts by Italian correspondents in
London, little is known here outside high military and
Royal quarters of the magnificent work done by our
new Armies and those of the Dominions at Fricourt,
Pozières, and Longueval.

In the highest Royal and military quarters interest,
confidence, and admiration are warmly expressed,
but unluckily Italian Parliamentary and business
circles and the bulk of the Army know nothing of the
meaning of our successes and sacrifices in the Somme
offensive. Their eyes are concentrated on Verdun
and the Russian fronts.

Yet the importance of thorough mutual compre-
hension here is manifest. The Isonzo is, so to speak,
the western Balkan front. Blows struck here are
felt in Sofia as well as in Vienna, and should encourage
the Allies at Salonica as well as in Galicia. Co-
ordination of Allied public opinion may be as important as co-ordination of military effort. It is
essential to complete victory that each of the Allies
should feel towards the others the trust and admiration which they all merit and which knowledge alone
can engender and maintain.

IV

ON THE CADORE FRONT

THE "WIRE WAYS"—A MOTOR DRIVE
IN AUSTRIA

ON THE CADORE FRONT, *August* 15.

ON Sunday afternoon I witnessed on the Isonzo front a prolonged bombardment, at a distance of 5,500 yards, of a rocky cavern in which an Austrian battery of mountain guns and a number of machine-guns were known to be concealed. Hour after hour 8 in. Howitzers planted their shells within a few yards of the same spot. It was bright and clear, and through a powerful telescope we could pick out every individual pine tree in the neighbourhood of the cavern, and see great rock splinters being thrown in all directions at the moment of the explosion of the shell.

This morning I am writing in brilliant sunshine and several degrees of frost on the Cadore front. It is not usually realized that the Italian front is nearly 500 miles long. In the parched, stony wilderness of the Carso, which I have already described, the chief enemy of the fighting man is thirst. The chief enemy on the Cadore front is frost. These two facts should bring home some of the difficulties that the Italians have faced for 15 months.

In discussing the peculiarities of the mountain fighting as contrasted with the fighting on the road to Trieste, his Majesty the King of Italy, who has a fine

sense of words, and who has spoken English from childhood, said :—" Picture to yourself my men 9,000 ft. up
in the clouds for seven months, in deep snow, so close
to the Austrians that at some points the men can see
their enemies' eyes through the observation holes.
Imagine the difficulties of such a life with continual
sniping and bomb-throwing."

King Victor Emmanuel's grim picture of war was
in such strong contrast to the tropical fighting round
Gorizia that I asked General Cadorna for permission
to come and see the fighting in the clouds. The
illustrated newspapers have from time to time published photographs of great cannon carried up into
these Dolomite Alps, but I confess to having never
realized what it means. It had never occurred to me
to imagine what happens to the wounded men, or to
the dead. How do supplies and ammunition reach
these lonely sentinels of our Allies ?

I have watched great steamers arrive at our British
bases in France—the transport of their freight by
train and the wonderful motor service, and then on by
light railways or horse vehicles. Here food for the
men and food for the guns go first by giddy, zigzag
roads, specially built by the Italians for this war.
They are not mere tracks, but are as wide as the Grand
Corniche that runs between Nice and Mentone, or the
Hog's Back between Guildford and Farnham. When
these have reached their utmost possible height there
comes a whole series of " wire ways," as the Italian
soldiers call them. Steel cables slung from hill to hill,
from ridge to ridge, span yawning depths and reach
almost vertically into the clouds. Up these cables go guns
and food, as well as timber for the huts, in which the
men live ; and material for entrenchments. Down
these come the wounded. The first sensation of a
transit down these seemingly fragile tight-ropes is
much more curious than the first trip in a submarine
or aeroplane, and tries even the strongest nerves.

Man is not only fighting man at these heights, but both Italians and Austrians have been fighting Nature in some of her fiercest aspects. The gales and snow-storms are excelled in horror by avalanches. Quite lately the melting snow revealed the frozen bodies, looking horribly lifelike, of a whole platoon which had been swept away nearly a year ago.

While there have been heavy casualties on both sides from sniping, bombing, mountain- and machine-guns, and heavy artillery, there has been little sickness among the Italians. The men know that doctors' visits are practically impossible. Therefore they fol-low the advice of their officers. King Victor Em-manuel, whose life has been passed almost entirely among the troops since the beginning of the war, told me, however, that despite the greatest care, occasional casualties from frost-bite are impossible to avoid. Yet the men have all the comforts that it is humanly possible to obtain. The cloud fighters are extremely well fed. Huts are provided, fitted with stoves similar to those used in Arctic expeditions.

I do not know how many kinds of artillery are used in these Alps. In addition to heavy guns there are guns carried on mules and guns partly carried by mountain artillerymen—huge fellows whose weight-carrying capacity entirely puts into the shade that of the Constantinople *hamels*, or porters. When Queen Margherita arrived at Gressoney some years ago, four Alpine gunners *presented arms with the guns of a battery*. They are cheery fellows, not a little proud of their strength, and with backs like bulls.

Higher yet than the mountain fighting line stand the vedettes, sentinels and outposts whose work re-sembles that of expert Alpine climbers. They carry portable telephones, with which they can communicate with their platoon. The platoon in turn telephones to the local commander. When thinking of our own brave men who have held the trenches in French

Flanders for these two years and who now, with
Dominion and Oversea troops, are alongside the
French slowly forcing back the Germans on the Somme,
it is only fair that we should realize that, but for the
work of these Italians in weakening Germany's chief
ally in the mountains, on the lower ground near
Gorizia, in Gorizia itself, and in the Carso desert,
our advance would not have been possible.

Proof of the Austrian expectation of swarming
down on to the rich Venetian plain is afforded by
documents recently captured giving the names of the
officers appointed as governors of such important
Italian cities as Vicenza.

Motoring through that luscious plain yesterday, with
its vineyards, mulberry trees, vast expanses of ripe
maize, its fat pastures and abundant orchards, one
could but rejoice at the chagrin of these dupes
of the German Kaiser. They had feasted their
eyes from afar on this beautiful scene. They had
been told in an Order of the Day that the
good wine and fair women of Italy awaited them.
Many, indeed, arrived on the plain—as prisoners—
and are now quarrelling among themselves as to who
brought disaster upon them. It is "those *verdammte*
Magyars," say the Austrians. It is "those Austrian
swine," say the Magyars.

I do not know the tale of prisoners taken by the
Italians, but I do know that almost daily at one
point or another I have found "cages" of them,
all well-fed and not altogether displeased at being
at last in the promised land.

Motoring in Austria in war time is most pleasing.
Italy holds a good deal more of Austria than seems
to be understood. No fewer than 500 Austrian com-
munes are already under Italian administration.
Austrian names have been removed from the streets,
Hamburg-Amerika advertisements have been painted
over, and Odol and Sanatogen are seen no more.

The black and yellow frontier posts and the *Tabak-trafiken* have been done away with, and only the comfortable Austrian Gasthäuser remain, though they are not overcrowded as formerly with German and Austrian tourists. If one could get permission, which I confess is difficult, I know nothing more agreeable than a visit to the Italian part of Austria in war time.

Yesterday I was in Cortina, where doubtless many readers of these lines have spent happy summer holidays. The Austrian bombardment seems to have ceased. Several reasons are given. One is that the Austrians thought it undesirable to go on killing the relatives of 800 Cortina soldiers in their ranks. Another is that the large hotels are chiefly owned by Austrians and are heavily mortgaged to Viennese banks. My own belief is that the cessation of the bombardment, which has wholly or partially smashed many hotels and buildings, is due to the slow crumbling of the Austrian offensive power to which I have referred.

V

FIGHTING IN THE DOLOMITES

TRENCHES 10,000 FEET UP

CADORE FRONT, *August* 16.

IN reading the steady flow of good news that has followed General Cadorna's great *coup de main*, it is important to bear in mind the several factors which have rendered it possible. First among them were the preparation and organization of the Italian Army, which to-day is as well equipped, trained, and organized as any of the Allied Armies. At the outset General Cadorna's troops lacked many things. The wars in Abyssinia and Libya had, indeed, taught them the value of good equipment, but they had to learn the requirements of modern European warfare in the hard school of actual war.

Italy is now throwing herself into the land war as heartily as is the British Empire. Many of her initial difficulties were not unlike our own. Others are peculiar to her geographical environment. The recent Italian successes on the Carso would have been impossible had not the mountain armies on the Trentino and the Cadore held a very large proportion of the total enemy forces, which at one moment numbered at least 800,000 men. Austria is compelled to keep many strong divisions on these mountain fronts lest numerical weakness should expose her to the cutting of some of her most important strategic railways, notably the Puster Valley railway, which runs eastward from the Tirolese fortress of Franzensfeste along the

Drave Valley, and is even now exposed at Toblach
to the long-range fire of the Italian heavy guns on
this Cadore front. She is therefore unable seriously
to reinforce either the armies which are retreating
before the Russians or those which are falling back
on the waterpipes in the Carso desert. It should
always be remembered that the Austrians have
waterpipes, which they destroy as they retreat,
whereas the Italians are handicapped by having to
construct them as they advance, just as we are
doing on the Somme.

General Cadorna is intensely grateful to the heroes
fallen in this strange, deadly guerilla warfare on the
mountain peaks. I saw yesterday one young officer
with three medals for valour. In one division alone
40 such medals were recently distributed—a sure sign
how General Cadorna, who is no sentimentalist,
appreciates the gallantry of these fighters among the
precipices and avalanches.

On reaching the headquarters of this division at
dawn I found a batch of prisoners captured in a
midnight battle near a Dolomite summit drawn up
in line. In contradistinction to the prisoners taken
in the Gorizia battle, they were ragged and unkempt
tramps. The only decent thing about them were
their boots, rifle, and the stout mountain staff which
each carried. The captors, with soldierly generosity, had
shared their own soup with them—food such as, the
prisoners said, they had not tasted for six months.
One had a lump of Austrian military bread. It is
before me as I write. Dark coloured—not the healthy
colour of rye bread—hard to chew, sodden to touch,
evil of smell, it seems barely possible that it can
sustain the strength of human beings in the coming
terrible winter conditions of this mountain warfare.

As the sun rose the great peaks of the Dolomites
stood out like pink pearls, set here and there in a
soft white vapour. Coming through a Canadian-

looking pine forest, with log-house barracks, kitchens, and canteens beneath one such peak, I was reminded of Dante's lines :—" Gazing above, I saw her shoulders clothed already with the planet's rays." But poetic memories soon faded before a sniper's bullet from a very near Austrian outlook.

At one spot the Austrian and Italian barbed wire entanglements were clearly visible through glasses on a neighbouring summit at a height of over 10,000 feet. A few yards below in an open cavern protected by an over-hanging rock the little grey tents of Italy's soldiers were plainly seen. It may be a consolation to our men on the Somme and in Flanders to know that the war is being waged here in conditions equally as dangerous as theirs.

The Italians have driven back the Austrians foot by foot up the almost vertical Dolomite rock with mountain, field, and heavy guns, and especially in hand-to-hand and bomb fighting. Sniping never ceases by day, but the actual battles are almost invariably fought by night.

The only day fighting is when, as in the famous capture of Col di Lana and more recently at Castelletto, the whole or part of a mountain top has to be blown off, because it is impossible to turn or carry it by direct assault. Tunnels, sometimes 800 yards long, are drilled by machinery through the solid rock beneath the Austrian strongholds, which presently disappear under the smashing influence of 30 or 40 tons of dynamite. Then the Alpini swarm over the *débris* and capture or kill the enemy survivors and rejoice in a well-earned triumph.

One needs to have scaled a mountain side to an Italian gun emplacement or look-out post to gauge fully the nature of this warfare. Imagine a catacomb, hewn through the hard rock, with a central hall and galleries leading to a gun position 7,000 feet up. Reckon that each gun emplacement represents three months' constant labour with drill, hammer, and mine. Every

requirement, as well as food and water, must be
carried up by men at night or under fire by day.
Every soldier employed at these heights needs another
soldier to bring him food and drink, unless, as happens
in some places, the devoted wives of the Alpini act
nightly under organized rules as porters for their
husbands.

The food supply is most efficiently organized. A
young London Italian private, speaking English
perfectly, whom I met by chance, told me, and I have
since verified the information, that the men holding
this long line of the Alps received special food,
particularly during the seven months' winter. Besides
the excellent soup which forms the staple diet of the
Italian as of the French soldiers, the men receive a
daily ration of two pounds of bread, half a pound of
meat, half a pint of red wine, macaroni of various
kinds, rice, cheese, dried and fresh fruit, chocolate,
and, thrice weekly, small quantities of Cognac and
Marsala.

Members of the Alpine Club know that in the high
Dolomites water is in summer often as precious as on
the Carso. Snow serves this purpose in winter.
Three months' reserve supplies of oil fuel, food, alcohol,
and medicine must be stored in the catacomb mountain
positions, lest, as happened to an officer whom I met,
the garrisons should be cut off by snow for weeks and
months at a time. I have already pointed out that
the Italians have driven the Austrians in most cases
by sheer hard fighting to the very tops of the peaks.
Unless the positions thus won were firmly held during
the winter they might rapidly be lost at the melting
of the snows. They form an essential portion of the
great Allied siege of Germany. Sir Douglas Haig
has asserted that the war is a young man's game.
Certainly, as far as concerns the fighting in the high
Alps, men above 30 are of very little use.

The experience of the Italian front brings into

prominence one little understood aspect of the Italian character—its patience, and its industry as of ants. *Pazienza* is one of the commonest Italian words. Here it is exemplified both by faith and works.

Its faith is wonderful. It believes whole-heartedly in the Allied cause. The men display the keenest admiration for the British Army. They are hungry for news of its doings. They are proud to be its Allies. I repeat that the Italian newspapers, which I scan daily for news from home, tell them little beyond Sir Douglas Haig's *communiqués*. Yet the Italian Press possesses some of the best popular writers of our time. The men in the lonely catacombs at the top of the Dolomites or struggling across the thirsty Carso would be consoled to know that their hardships and perils are fully shared by their British brothers in arms, who side by side with the French are fighting in the trenches, on the Somme, and in Flanders.

The work of our Navy is entirely understood in Italy, but I repeat with emphasis that the superb work of our Army needs to be made known.

VI

THE GATE TO ITALY BARRED

Roads versus Big Guns

Trentino Front, *August* 17.

Autumn leaves were swirling at Asolo, a charming spot reminiscent of the Brownings, as we passed through yesterday on the way to this front, the scene of so much ghastly fighting during the Austrian offensive and its repulse.

The Kaiser has sown his dragon's teeth well. All through this beautiful province of Venetia are soldiers drilling, soldiers marching, infantry, Alpini, cavalry, motor transport, ammunition columns, big guns, and field guns. Women, who look as though they had walked out of Titian's pictures, are gathering the third harvest. Old men and boys—a hundred and twenty thousand of them on this part of the front alone—are making and repairing the wonderful roads that lead to victory. Fig, apple, peach, and olive trees, vines, maize, noble villas, tall campanili, 15th century façades—one has the impression of travelling through whole picture galleries of great Venetian masters. The heat in the Plain is terrific.

Climbing by the new war roads to an altitude of 5,000 ft., we came upon a front not unlike that of the Somme, with the difference that the ground is covered by a vast amount of rock and stone, even in the woods were then hostile armies facing each other. Crawling, in order not to draw the enemy artillery, to the edge of one of these woods, which is almost as utterly

P

destroyed as Mametz, we looked across an apparently peaceful upland valley, difficult to associate with war unless examined with glasses, which reveal ruined houses, villages, and churches.

Here the Italians recently repulsed 360,000 Austrians equipped with 26 batteries of 12-inch guns. The fighting in this region presents, as it does on every front, its own particular difficulties. Aeroplane observation is both difficult and dangerous, owing to the presence of vast scattered rocks, with little landing space. Trenches must here, as in the Cadore and Carso, be drilled by machinery and blasted. The Austrians are well provided with petrol-driven machine drills. With these they also excavate deep caverns for hiding the guns. One lately captured was unusually light and strong, with a new type of Mercédès engine.

What I may call the Prisoner Puzzle is accentuated by the fact that the prisoners recently taken here are of remarkably fine physique, unlike those I saw yesterday. They are mostly Austrian-Germans, Poles, and Ruthenes.

The effect of high explosive shells here is unusually terrible. Splinters from the rocks and stones seriously increase the efficacy of the projectile. A young Italian, who at the beginning of the war joined the French Army as a volunteer and was wounded at Verdun, recovered and has since fought here, said :—" At Verdun the big shell is a big shell ; among these rocks it is equal to 10 big shells." Fortunately, the same applies to the Italian shells fired against the Austrians, who have their own tale of woe to tell.

The various sectors of the Trentino front have been described more frequently and adequately than any other part of the Italian line. I will not repeat those descriptions, but seek to convey an idea of the problem imposed upon his soldiers by General Cadorna when the great Austrian 12-inch guns suddenly began last May. Against the concentration of the Austrian artillery monsters and masses of infantry the Italians were for the moment powerless. Though holding well on both flanks, in the centre the Italians were overwhelmed and their bases of supply disorganized. Could the foe be stopped before reaching the Plain ? Already his shells were bursting along the southernmost brow of the Sette Comuni plateau. Asiago and Arsiero were taken. Schio and Vicenza seemed within grasp. The problem resolved itself into one of time. A few hours might turn the scale.

The full story of the rapid concentration of Italian forces, the organization of fresh bases of supply, including water, of which there is none on the Asiago plateau, and particularly the problem of the conversion of mountain mule-tracks overnight into splendid motor roads cannot yet be told. When told it will form one of the most thrilling chapters of the war. It was roads *versus* big guns. Roads won. In face of the strengthening of the Italian counter-pressure the Austrians hesitated to bring forward their heavy batteries. Hesitation proved fatal to their plans. The completion of the roads enabled General Cadorna to hold them, to baffle them, until the Russian offensive prevented the Austrians from making good their severe losses, and relieved the pressure on the Italians. The only door into Italy was slammed in the enemy's face. Now it is bolted and barred. I saw the bars yesterday. They are stout.

The Italian commander who now holds the gate does not under-estimate the enemy. He is a keen, hard, experienced soldier, with a splendid staff. He has no illusions as to the effort required, but knows that the foe will be beaten. " We may knock fragments off the Austrian mass here and there," he said,

" but we must go on hammering until we and others smash the whole block of Hapsburg concrete to atoms."

On my way back from the outer edge of the wood, well within the fire zone, I visited one of the Italian surgical mobile hospitals with an operating theatre that can be folded and carried by motor. It is used only for urgent stomach and head wounds that cannot bear delay or removal. A portable X-ray apparatus, a motor water-wagon carrying 500 gallons, four nurses, four surgeons, physicians, and orderlies complete the equipment. During the last two months 240 urgent operations have been performed. The hospital has 200 beds. It was given by the city of Milan and works under the Italian Red Cross.

I have visited several other hospitals. All are in every respect modern, well staffed, and well equipped. The complete absence of flies is a remarkable feature of the Italian hospitals. I wish to call attention to the splendid work done by the British Red Cross hospitals near Cormons, to which are attached 24 ambulances. This and other ambulance sections are highly spoken of by the Italians, who regard the British Red Cross activity as a pleasing manifestation of Allied sympathy.

Lord Monson is in charge and Sir Courtauld Thomson is now on a visit of inspection and is highly satisfied. Much good work has also been done by the Fourth Section of the British Red Cross, which has a travelling X-ray car under the management of two English ladies, Countess Helen Gleichen and Mrs. Hollings. Owing to hard work during the battle of Gorizia one car has been put out of action, but I suggest the provision of another car specially constructed for mountain climbing, such as is made by the Italian Fiat Company. The value of the work of the Fourth Section can be gathered by the fact that as many as 60 urgent cases have been radiographed, often under fire, in a single day. All the Red Cross work here presents unusual difficulties, owing to the heat and the lack of water.[1]

What is evident here is that the whole of industrial Italy is being mobilized for war, as is industrial Britain, and that the Italians are as much in earnest as are the British.

On this, as on other parts of the front, the horrible conduct of the Austrians and Hungarians in using explosive bullets and iron-spiked bludgeons for killing the wounded has intensified the war feeling. Austrians, like Germans, make reprisals for defeats in the field by acts of cruelty and vandalism. Thus, as a reply to the defeat at Gorizia, the Austrians attempted to destroy St. Mark's at Venice. The enemy here is symbolized by Francis Joseph, whose portrait is often found roughly but cleverly sketched on the walls or hanged in paper effigy on the lamps. He is known to the Italians, not as a venerable old man borne down by family sorrows, but as shrewd, hard, imperious, and impervious to all family bereavements.

In leaving the Italian Armies, I desire to point out that accredited visitors are allowed to make any enquiry they choose and see everything they desire, and that the censorship is extremely light and strictly military. General Cadorna's view is that if anything is wrong it should be made known, so that it may speedily be put right. Personally, I have been allowed every kind of freedom.

The only regret I have felt during a rapid and incomplete survey of the reawakening of the old martial spirit of Italy concerns the absence of propaganda in regard to the part that the British Empire is playing. It is only by the reciprocal knowledge of the achievement of each Ally that we shall get

[1] The car was provided.

the fullest effort and enthusiasm from all. Those to whom I have given information privately as to the real number of our fighting men in France and elsewhere, of our output of shells and big guns, and of the successive capturing of the German colonial possessions are astounded. Parliamentary figures giving percentages carry no weight.

I have been greatly helped in my pleasant task of recording a little of Italy's efforts by the kindness of his Majesty King Victor Emmanuel, who is the Commander-in-Chief of the Italian armies, their Excellencies Generals Cadorna and Porro, Colonel Clericetti, and Captain Pirelli, and many other officers.

Brigadier-General Delmé-Radcliffe, head of the British Military Mission at Italian Headquarters, whose acquaintance with military Italy is probably unique and who seems able to dispense with sleep and is at his desk or in the field 18 hours daily, provided me with the most efficient assistance and with information without which my work could not have been done, nor my most interesting visit arranged.

NEUTRAL GLIMPSES

I

THE GERMANS IN SWITZERLAND

ZÜRICH, SWITZERLAND

ON leaving Italy I spent some days in Switzerland en route for Spain, and was able to gather a good deal of miscellaneous information not without value.

At night, Zürich, the first large neutral city in which I have been since the beginning of the war, is as bright as London was in July, 1914. Rome, too, is bright, but over the Italian capital there is the indefinable atmosphere of war.

In coming up through the Swiss-Italian lakes, we were at once among German tourists. At Lugano we saw figures familiar enough before the war, the stout, elderly German husband, followed at a respectful distance by his wife in her atrocious *Reformkleid*. It was like going back years in one's life. In the train were Germans who talked loudly at us, and stared in the German way. The dining-car was filled with the usual German advertisements; rather amusingly some of them read to-day—the Hamburg-Amerika Linie with an illuminated picture of one of Herr Ballin's ocean monsters on its way to New York!

It was near midnight when we reached Zürich. One remembers only the German voices, the electric brightness of the streets, and the familiar rushing

of the river. But it felt like Germany. Next morning, as we woke after delightful sleep induced by
much journeying, the impression was for a moment
that of a nightmare. Was it Germany, or was
it not ? On the floor, where it had been disrespectfully
thrown over night, was the big eiderdown *Federdecke*.
At my right hand on the wall was a prominent
notice in large German type :—

> *Die Zimmerpreise werden erhöht wenn keine
> der Hauptmahlzeiten im Hotel genommen wird,
> auch wenn der Preis vorher festgesetzt.*

The waiter who brings the coffee speaks German
only.

Looking down into the sunny street at seven in
the morning, we see a German town alive and busy,
new, spick and span, like most German cities. The
Städtische Strassenbahnen are packed with business
men. School children are pouring through the streets
and across the squares. There are the little girls
with spectacles, double pigtails and knapsacks ; big
boys with spectacles, socks, and bare legs ; students
with queer caps.

Zürich is efficient. It is obviously well managed.
There are almost as many " Achtung " and " Ver-
boten " signs as in Hanover itself. It is so efficient
that the little people are dragged out of their beds
and sent to school at seven in the morning—an hour
when other little people in a less over-organized
country are prattling and bathing as children should.
At night they are still about at a very late hour.

All English people have a strange sensation when
first walking through a German neutral town in war
time. Little but German is heard. The old familiar
" Delikatessen " and " Bier vom Fass " notices in-
tensify the feeling. This part of German Switzerland,
though by no means hostile towards individual Britons
or, indeed, towards the Empire, is completely German.

In Zürich the English traveller finds himself cheek by jowl with our chief enemy, for the *Reichsdeutsch* population of Zürich is large. These " Imperial Germans " are not, as a rule, offensive, and are considerably more civil to the English than they were before the war.

The attitude of the German-Swiss was, naturally, anti-Ally at first, but it is becoming less and less hostile, and, in some ways, positively appreciative. These same good people of Zürich, who strike the British visitor as being so German, recently besieged the railway station to welcome the passing British prisoners on their way to hospitable internment. At some places barriers were erected to keep back the crowds who assembled in thousands merely to see the trains pass in the middle of the night, and to cheer the newcomers. At Zürich the police were powerless, and the enthusiasm for the wounded British was delirious. These manifestations of Swiss good-heartedness have quite obliterated from the minds of British residents the memory of the rough handling to which some were subjected at the beginning of the war. Even those who, like *The Times* Correspondent, were arrested and kept in custody for various periods warmly recognize the friendliness of the Swiss people.

The German-Swiss, I think, are puzzled about the war, and especially about Verdun. On the bookstalls you find side by side with more modest collections of *The Times* and of the Continental Edition of the *Daily Mail*, suspicious great piles of the *Frankfurter Zeitung*, the *Vossische Zeitung*, the *Neue Freie Presse*, and of all the chief German and Austrian newspapers.

These same German and Austrian journals and their German-Swiss contemporaries gave great prominence to the Kaiser's famous February despatch, in which he stated that his brave Branden-

burgers had stormed the " fortress of Douaumont,"
and suggested that Douaumont was a real fortress
commanding the ruined little city on the Meuse.

As I pointed out in a message telegraphed to *The
Times* from Verdun early in March, and reprinted
in this volume, Douaumont is a fort only in name.
Six months have now elapsed, and the German-Swiss
see that all the military might of their kinsmen
has been without avail. The French-Swiss newspapers, in good Fleet-street style, are " rubbing
it in." They reprint the February headlines of the
German newspapers and passages from an eminent
German military critic who wrote :—

> Verdun is at its last gasp. Even as I write
> our brave troops are probably quartered in its
> houses.

The only reply from Germany is the monotonous
and outworn suggestion that the reduction of Verdun
is taking its normal course.

It should be borne in mind that the business
connexions and family ties between Germany and
German Switzerland are nearly as close as those
between England and Scotland. Yet some of the
German-Swiss newspapers are fair and give both
sides a hearing. This is the more remarkable, since
German propaganda by bribed newspaper, kinematograph, advertisement, private letter, business threat
and bribe never ceases. Through her hosts of secret
agents Germany hears when this or that citizen of
German Switzerland has expressed unorthodox views.
Within a few hours the culprit receives a private
letter carefully controverting his opinions.

German methods of working upon neutrals have
often been analyzed, but I think the most effective
of them are still news-twisting and rapidity of
publication. In the train between Zürich and Berne
one bull-necked Hun of the commercial traveller

ype read, too loudly to be polite, a German report
of the most recent North Sea "scrap," not a word
about which had arrived from London. As before,
the idea of our losses was allowed to remain in the
German, Austrian, and neutral mind long enough
to become embedded there.

Comparison with our belated Admiralty report
next day showed that the German *communiqué* was
an artful piece of lying, but the lie had a long start,
as in the Jutland battle matter.

Another object of the German propaganda is
to give the impression that affairs in Germany
are going on as usual. Throughout Switzerland
the great German steamship advertisements appear
as though the Atlantic were still open. The Hamburg-Amerika offices in the various towns look
as if nothing had changed. The Balkan-Zug (Balkan
Express) has flaring advertisements and time-tables
posted up on the walls of stations showing its route
" Berlin-Budapest-Sofia-Konstantinopel." I saw one
of them purposely placed beside a modest announcement of the Great Western Railway " the route
for England's most historic sites and Cathedral
Cities."

There are some faint efforts at British propaganda.
They might be greatly improved upon and intensified.
Our " man in the street " may ask why we should
trouble at all about German Switzerland or Switzerland in general, but Downing-street, I imagine,
has reason to know otherwise. Nor would Germany
be putting in propaganda seven days a week unless
she had certain objects in view.

In French Switzerland our French Allies are rendering
us great services. They have organized at Geneva a
series of lectures upon " The Effort of the Allies " by
eminent French writers and statesmen. The Germans
have striven to undermine Swiss belief in Allied cohesion.
With true French insight, our friends saw that if France

bore generous witness to what her Allies have done
and are doing, her assurance would carry greater
weight than any assurance which individual Allies
could give on their own behalf. The result has been
a series of manifestations of which the effect is not
confined to French Switzerland.

French Switzerland is more fervently and, as I
gathered at a public meeting, more vociferously pro-
Ally than are some of the Allied countries themselves.
German Switzerland is sentimentally pro-German, but,
as I have said, is striving to be fair. But Switzerland
as a whole is pro-Swiss " first, last, and all the
time," as the Americans say.

Of Italian Switzerland I saw little, but I gathered
that notwithstanding some misapprehensions, there
is a general feeling of relief at the knowledge that
the completion of the defences on the Italian side
of the frontier has diminished any temptation which
Germany may have felt to violate Swiss neutrality
in that direction. Switzerland is naturally afraid
of Germany and knows her well enough to understand
that no sentimental consideration would protect
Swiss neutrality, did a definite military advantage
seem obtainable. Every step taken by France or
Italy to deprive the Germans in advance of such
an advantage, therefore, enhances the security of
the Swiss.

Au fond des choses, I believe it is the championship
of the cause of little nations by England in the past
and by the Allies in the present that has most affected
the attitude of Switzerland. The war has chastened
her and has caused her to realize her comparative
helplessness. " You are becoming absolutely Ger-
manized," I said to a young bank manager who was
changing some money for me. " Not at all," he
replied. " We admire Germany, but her rule would
be too rigid for us free Republicans. We are grateful
to England for her protection of small nations,

but we fear Russia. We have not forgotten Russia's visit of a hundred years ago."

His was a very different tone from that of a German, straight from Frankfurt, with the *Frankfurter Zeitung* in his hand, a member of the race which has made Frankfurt famous. He was an elderly man, and opened the conversation in fairly respectable English by asking if I came from England. He proceeded to show me that he knew nothing whatever about the war.

I should have expected this attitude from an ordinary German, but here was a Jew, a member of one of the most intelligent races of the world, a race that has been given quick powers of insight, inference, and deduction. Yet he was convinced that Germany had been basely attacked, that the English Navy was paralyzed, that London was almost in ruins, that England was on her last legs financially and on the eve of a social revolution, that Hindenburg was cunningly drawing Brusiloff and the Russians on to their doom.

Nor was the man without knowledge of England. He had been there twice—in London once and once in the Isle of Wight. He was especially loud in his lamentations over our futile attempt " to starve the women and children in Germany," but had nothing to say when I pointed out how Bismarck had treated Paris in 1870. He was also particularly angry that the Swiss should be making fuzes for our shells, and said that the Swiss were as bad as the Americans. I explained that neutral countries had often done this kind of thing and that the Swiss, by the way, were making aluminium for the German Zeppelins, in whose future potentialities the old gentleman had infinite belief. He was especially eloquent over the condition of German finance and the relatively good position of the mark in Switzerland.

I asked him if he ever read the English *communiqués*, which, by the way, seem to be very fully given in the German Press. He replied that he did, but they were all lies. Verdun, of course, was going all right. Germany, he admitted, was suffering from lack of several kinds of food and raw material. He confessed that he was glad of the opportunity of getting a few days in such a land of plenty as that in which he was travelling. He thought the war would last at least till Christmas, at which time France would have collapsed and England would be asking to be allowed to " go home," to use his own words. Germany would not be ungenerous. " I am not an annexationist," he added. " It will be enough if we retain Antwerp and some control over the manufacturing districts of France and Belgium, with freedom of the seas, and big compensation for ill-treatment of the German colonies, *plus* means to complete the direct route from Antwerp, Berlin, Constantinople, and Baghdad, with a port at the end of the line."

The Swiss are better informed than this. They know more of the true position and hear constantly of the cross-currents in Germany. Swiss workmen have recently returned from Germany in considerable numbers. They prefer the lower wages and the full meals of Helvetia to the high pay and low diet of Prussia. They have heard of the peace feelers constantly thrown out, not only by the German Imperial Government, but by some of the Governments of the Federal States. But they have not, and cannot have, a clear idea of the determination that animates all the Allies, and their very neutrality clouds their perception of the full meaning of the war.

How wide is the gulf that separates belligerent from neutral countries is revealed almost painfully to visitors by the presence of large numbers of young

men in the streets. In Rome there are still some,
but they are going daily. In Paris there are none.
Thus when one comes first to a neutral country
the great space which youth occupies in the social
landscape is instantly revealed. The departure of
our youth for camp and battlefield is part, a large
part, of the price we are paying for our freedom;
but it is a singular fact that, despite the presence
of young men, the atmosphere of neutrality is
depressing.

When passports have been examined at the French
frontier stations, and the familiar light blue uniforms
once more predominate, one will breathe again.
In these great days the breath of war is the breath
of life, and the spirit of sacrifice is the spirit of
regeneration.

II

OUR RELEASED PRISONERS

Happy as Schoolboys

MÜRREN, SWITZERLAND

The topsy-turveydoms of war are many.

Just after the Battle of the Marne I witnessed the curious spectacle of a number of slightly-wounded brawny Highlanders exchanging remarks with the passers-by from the windows of one of the most exclusive hotels in the world, the Bristol, at the corner of the Place Vendôme, in Paris, long the resort of Kings and others of high degree.

To-day, here at Mürren, in the most beautiful spot in all Switzerland, I am watching two British bluejackets looking through a telescope at a distant eyrie, in which a couple of young eaglets can be plainly seen, the great parent birds wheeling and swooping like a pair of more graceful aeroplanes.

The bluejackets, with between four and five hundred officers and men of his Majesty's Army, are prisoners of war, interned here, and interned, I may say, in the very lap of luxury.

Accompanied by Colonel Picot, ex-Military Attaché to our Legation in Switzerland, we set out early this morning on one of the most delightful motor rides imaginable, through the Bernese Oberland, by Thun, its towering schloss and emerald lake, to Lauterbrunnen. Tirol itself affords no greater delights to the eye. All is German, of course; the inns, Gasthäuser zum Loewen, Adler, and the like, and the

Q 2

motor signs :—" Achtung ! " and the very necessary
" Achtet auf die Kinder "—for the roads swarm with
flaxen-headed tots.

Here and there are the unexpected contrast of
French *poilus*, in their *bleu d'horizon*, fishing, flirting,
strolling in groups, or cycling, but generally fishing,
and with greater result than in the Seine or the *lac*
in the Bois de Boulogne, for they hold up to us great
trout, pike, and " omble chevalier "—the last a fish new
to me.

These are the French interned prisoners in
Switzerland. Unlike our men, who are at present
chiefly at two centres, Château d'Oex and Mürren,
the French are scattered in little companies throughout
the Oberland. There are one-eyed, one-legged, and
one-armed men, but they have all escaped from the
Horror.

Presently we come to Interlaken, and soon at
Lauterbrunnen we take the steep mountain railway
up to this delectable assemblage of hotels and chalets,
in which our soldiers, broken in the war, are being
rapidly restored to health by the healing air and sunshine of these higher Alps.

Colonel Neish received us at the little station, and
in a few minutes we are in the midst of as great a war
contrast as can be imagined.

Almost everyone knows Mürren, but for those who
have not that pleasure I will say that it is on a little
plateau, immediately facing what many people regard
as the most beautiful mountain in Europe, the Jungfrau. Within view are the Wetterhorn, the Eiger,
the Mönch.

By an arrangement with the Swiss Government,
who have behaved as kindly to our poor men as have
the Swiss people themselves—which is saying a great
deal—the soldiers who were taken at Mons and at
Le Cateau, at Loos, and some even more recently,
are housed in the very best mountain hotels and

chalets in Switzerland. The men only arrived at
Mürren last week, and have not yet settled down to
freedom. Many of them still wear the strange look
noticeable in those who have got out of Germany.
Numbers can hardly yet realize that they are free, and
more than one remarked that when he awoke in the
morning in his comfortable bedroom, and gazed out
upon the brilliant sunshine on the snowy expanses
opposite, he feared it was but a dream.

For the whole of the general arrangements we have
to thank Colonel Hauser, the Swiss P.M.O. Mürren
and its region is in charge of a young Swiss medical
officer, Captain Llopart. Our prisoners, of course, are
under Swiss discipline, and our officers and non-
commissioned officers only hold their rank by courtesy
of the Swiss authorities. So far this extremely delicate
arrangement has worked admirably.

Colonel Neish, who looks and says he feels like a boy
out of school, after his long imprisonment, escorted
me at once to the Swiss officer in command, and we
then made an inspection of the village. Inasmuch
as most of the hotels and chalets have been built for
winter sports visitors from England, they are quite
new. And if there be any more sumptuously housed
privates in the British Army in any other part of the
world, I should be greatly surprised.

A man from hateful Wittenberg was lying in a deck-
chair on the sunny verandah outside his bedroom, to
which was attached the very latest type of private
bathroom. There was a bowl of roses and edelweiss
and a box of Woodbines by his side. He was getting
stronger, he said, as he stood to attention and saluted
Colonel Neish and Captain Llopart. By his bedside
I noticed a photograph of the wife and children at
home, and he had abundance of books and English
newspapers.

His surroundings are typical of all those at Mürren.
Nothing can be too good for our soldiers, and at

Mürren, and also at Château d'Oex, of which I obtained full accounts from English visitors, the best that modern hotels-de-luxe can give is given them. Flowers, sleep, sunshine, and happiness are everywhere.

The officers are housed separately, as are, of course, the non-commissioned officers. All the hotels are on the same scale of comfort, and there is therefore no difference of treatment.

At Château d'Oex work is in full swing, and the little colony at Mürren is already settling down into some form of discipline. When they first arrived, such as were able to walk clambered up and down the rambling mountain paths, shouting and singing like children on a school treat. They could with difficulty bring themselves to believe that they were free. Lately brothers in affliction, all were now enjoying the first taste of liberty, and liberty in the nearest approach to an earthly paradise that can be found in Europe.

Organization is steadily growing. Tailor soldiers have started a tailor shop. There is a library, in charge of a sergeant, and a barber's establishment. All who are able are beginning to help in such matters as waiting, washing up, and domestic assistance generally. The meals are exactly the same as those served to summer and winter visitors at Swiss mountain resorts. For breakfast : coffee, rolls, and honey. A substantial mid-day dinner of the best : good Swiss soup, roast mutton, roast beef, plenty of vegetables and fruit, plain puddings and compôtes. For supper : bread, cheese, jam, and everything in unlimited quantities. *The men need it.* Some are increasing in weight at a rate that seems almost incredible. All who are able to be out in the healing sunshine are getting sunburnt. There seems to be little desire for alcohol among them, but they can purchase, if they will, the light Swiss beer with which many of us have quenched our thirst in our holiday climbs.

Happiness is contagious.   One of the most pleasing moments in my recent very varied itinerary is this day among the prisoners of Mürren.   Each has his own tale to tell of life in Germany, and each will remember as long as he lives.   It is not the immediate policy of the British Government to emphasize German cruelties, and so I will not repeat the innumerable stories I have heard.

The particular sailormen at Mürren do not appear to have been badly used in Germany.   One young bluejacket from the Hebrides told me in his Highland accent that his life in Germany " might have been better and might have been worse."   An engineer from the *Appam*, captured by the *Moewe*, said that the captain of the *Moewe* was a thorough sportsman and a gentleman, and that his treatment in Germany had been fair.   It is not wise to generalize, but from the conversations I have had with sailors at Mürren, it would appear that, in their case, at any rate, different treatment was dealt out to sailors.

I heard other good things about Germany too. Among the many acts of self-sacrifice of the war is that of the distinguished Liverpool dental surgeon, Mr. J. A. W. Woods, who has given up his practice and come out to Mürren to look after the prisoners' teeth.   He told me that several of his patients had had good dental attention in Germany, and that in some cases false teeth had been given them.   Of other cases the less said the better.

For games there is a bowling alley, and such officers as are able to play have put the lawn tennis courts in order.   But at the present time most of them are more inclined to laze and read and get well.   Many are veritable Rip Van Winkles. Entirely shut off from news in Germany, except such fragments as they received from more recently arrived prisoners, they even now know practically nothing of what has happened since they were captured, and when I asked if there was any kind of reading they would care to have, the invariable reply was that they wanted histories of the war, especially those with illustrations. These I have arranged that they shall receive as speedily as possible.

As our interned men recover health, the question of their employment in Switzerland will become pressing. The whole subject is indeed fraught with difficulties, which are being solved as they arise, by the energy, knowledge, and tact of Colonel Picot, than whom a more suitable selection could not have been made. A British officer of world-wide experience and, as I said, late Military Attaché to our Legation, he understands the views of the Swiss and also those of our own men. The question is complicated by the fact that while so many of the Swiss factories are making munitions, it is forbidden, of course, that British or German soldiers interned in Switzerland should take part in such work. The Swiss Labour leaders, who naturally guard their own interests jealously, do not desire that the local labour market should be disturbed by what may prove to be an army of invading workers. The matter has already been dealt with in a special article in *The Times*, and I would merely say that at present the decision as to whether a man should or should not be allowed to enter a factory is decided by a local committee on which sit masters and men.

For the moment, I repeat, the great object is to get our prisoners well, and to that end Colonel Hauser and Colonel Picot work untiringly.

The Swiss peasants in this part of the country are well accustomed to English people. They have had summer incursions of our tourists for years, and the winter sports have lately taken us there in great numbers. In a way, our *internés* constitute a material boon to districts which have hitherto lived almost entirely on visitors. Our men are free with their money, and as many of the little shops are open, quite a trade is being done in lace, picture post-cards, and the usual souvenirs that tempt the shilling from the pocket.

To help the men to get well, English, French, and Swiss visitors come to amuse them, and those officers and men who are fit enough are helping with concerts, theatricals, and dances. Colonel Neish has told me that much is due to Mr. Lunn, who, twice rejected for military service at home, is doing good work in bringing peace of mind and of body to the lately released captives.

Up till now, at Mürren the novelty of the varying aspect of the Alps is almost sufficient entertainment. Perhaps not half-a-dozen of the men have ever been in real mountains before, and they are much surprised when told of the great distances separating them from points which in this clear atmosphere seem but a few miles away. They spend much of their time peering through glasses and telescopes at the glaciers and peaks. The blood-red sunset effect on the Jungfrau, famous throughout the world, has amazed them.

The officers are hoping, when they get well enough, to bag a chamois or two. The eyrie of the eagles to which I have referred is as great a pleasure to the local mountaineers as to our men, for they say that eagles long ago disappeared from this part of Switzerland. They look upon their return as a lucky omen. It is attributed by some among them to the Italian-Austrian bombardment of the Dolomites, but I am not learned in eagle lore, and merely give this statement for what it is worth.

Has the Mürren rose a thorn? For some of the men it has. Some 17 per cent. of them are married. The wives of some of the interned officers have already come out to stay with their husbands. The French

8

2 AT THE WAR

soldiers have their wives with them. It is too
much to expect that the Canadians, of whom there
are a number, should be able to transport their wives
from the other side of the Atlantic. But the words—
" I want to look upon my wife's face again "—very
sadly and earnestly spoken by one of the Old Army,
one of the heroes of Mons, were echoed in every hotel
and chalet I inspected.[1]

The cost of bringing out the wives on a visit is but
£12 each. Dare I suggest that, if Mr. Lloyd George
and the Treasury do not see their way to a very
trifling precedent, the British Red Cross Society
should satisfy this earnest wish of those who, in the
national cause, have been through the hell of the
trenches and the bottomless pit of the German prison
camps ?

[1] Charitable people at home at once provided the needed funds,
and at the time of writing parties of wives are being escorted to
Switzerland by British Red Cross Society representatives.

III

FOOD FOR OUR MEN IN GERMANY

*[The fine work described in this chapter has now
been partly superseded by Sir Starr Jameson's great
organization. I retain my description of it in justice
to those who did such great service for our prisoners
during many long months.]*

BERNE

MUCH that I heard at Mürren induced me to make
a few enquiries on the fringe of the great question
of the lot of our prisoners now languishing in the
hands of the enemy. It is an admittedly difficult
subject which has not yet been thoroughly grasped
and dealt with by the Government, even after more
than two years of war. But from the prisoners'
point of view one aspect of the problem is simple
enough. What they want and appreciate more than
anything else in their life of captivity is Bread.

Both in *The Times* and in the *World's Work*
my colleague of *The Times*, Gerald Campbell,
has given many interesting particulars of the steps
taken to meet this need by the British Section of
the Bureau de Secours aux Prisonniers de Guerre,
an admirable organisation established at Berne by
Lady Grant Duff, the gifted wife of the (then) British
Minister. The importance of the work and the call for
its further development are, however, alike so great
that it seems to me a matter of real national
interest to return to it once again.

The question of remittances of clothes, bread and other foods, and money is in so many hands at home that while it is more than possible that certain of our friendless prisoners in Germany get nothing, others, as I gather from statements made to me by released men at Mürren, get so much that they sell gifts, exchange them, or otherwise dispose of them to their guardians.

Bread is sent in large quantities direct from England. The released men with whom I conversed prefer the bread baked at Berne under the watchful eye of the president of the Bureau, her honorary secretary, an American gentleman, Mr. P. Grand d'Hauteville ; and Mr. and Mrs. Jebb Scott, honorary managers of the actual Bread Depot of this vast development.

The Berne bread reaches Germany more quickly and arrives in a better state than that from England. In appearance it resembles good French *pain de ménage*. It keeps, according to one of my informants, in wholesome condition for at least three weeks. I personally partook of it, both new and old. One Tommy criticized it as being too full of holes—" like Gruyère cheese," he said—but it is this very aeration that maintains its sweetness. Our soldiers in Germany call it " Burn " bread, this being their pronunciation of Berne. Most of them will remember with gratitude the name of the Swiss capital for the rest of their lives.

Owing to the fact that private donors are sometimes sending bread and sometimes forgetting to send it, and that there are numbers of excellent organizations at work in England apparently in ignorance of each other's operations, there is a certain amount of overlapping. There would be much more were it not for the practical and business-like system of the Berne Bureau, the energies of which are mainly devoted to checking and re-checking the various lists as they arrive from England.

The entire staff, which commenced rather more than a year ago with two people, now numbers 160 workers, paid or voluntary. For our prisoners in Bulgaria and Turkey, who are also dealt with by the Bureau staff—which includes our able Military Attaché, Lieutenant-Colonel W. F. G. Wyndham, M.V.O., Mr. R. J. A. Clarke, and Mr. L. Buchman, late Consul-General at Munich—special biscuits are baked, resembling a species of rusk or *Zwieback*.

There being no surplus of flour in Switzerland the prisoners' bread is made from a weekly supply of fifty tons, which by courtesy of the Swiss Government the Bureau is allowed to import from Marseilles. In this matter the Swiss have again behaved well. The Post Office, which carries the parcels, letters and post-cards, charges nothing for the service, nor do the railways for the carriage of the flour and the loaves and other parcels which go to Frankfurt. The German Government also carries these parcels free, a concession which is perhaps not to be wondered at since our national generosity relieves them of a great responsibility.

The chain of operations is as follows :—First, regimental committees or members of the public in all parts of the Empire send cheques or postal orders to the secretary of the organization, addressed to 50, Thunstrasse, Berne. The donors should send the names of the prisoners, with their regimental numbers, rank, and regiment, and the name of the camp or hospital in Germany, Bulgaria, or Turkey in which they are interned. Money-orders are a source of trouble to the organization, and it is especially requested that only cheques or postal-orders should be sent. Once the money has been received, for each sum of 4s., 4 lb. of bread are forwarded weekly for a month, strongly and neatly packed in ventilated cardboard " cartons." The bread reaches the prisoner sometimes within two or three days, and it rarely takes more than six days. A receipt post-card is enclosed in each parcel, and an advice postcard informing the prisoner that the bread has been dispatched and giving, if desired, the name of the person from whom it comes, is posted separately. From the replies received it is calculated that ninety-eight per cent. of the bread arrives safely and in good condition. At the present moment about 25,000 parcels of bread and other comforts of life are sent from Berne weekly to nearly 20,000 prisoners.

Personally, from things I have heard, I should be inclined to send help specially to " friendless " prisoners in Germany—men whose names are not included in any private or regimental list. Anyone who wishes to provide for prisoners of this class—there is a wide choice of British, Canadians, Australians, or Indians—is requested by the Berne people to apply to one of the regimental committees at home; in all cases the Bureau has found that it is more satisfactory to deal with these committees than with individuals.

How great is the need for bread was demonstrated to me by a released prisoner, who showed me the daily German bread ration that he had received. The specimen, which measures 6 in. long, 2 in. wide, and 2 in. thick, will be sent to England, where it will doubtless form a piece of propaganda in that man's part of the country for many a long year. He informed me, by the way, that the fifty-two disloyal members of the Irish Brigade are getting bread, despite their favoured treatment by the enemy.

It is not only bread, however, that goes from Berne. Here is a list of parcels which the Bureau de Secours undertakes to send direct to British prisoners of war in Germany on receipt of the necessary funds. Parcels are standardized, and the cost and contents are as follows :—

PARCEL A.—4s.

1 Alp milk chocolate
1 condensed milk
1 jam
1 cheese
1 block chocolate
2 packets tobacco
2 packets citrol
2 handkerchiefs or
1 hand towel or
1 housewife
1 tin Liebig

PARCEL B.—4s.

¼lb. tea
1 condensed milk
¼lb. lump sugar
1 jam
1lb. biscuits
1 block chocolate
6 Maggi soups
1 packet tobacco
1 towel

PARCEL C.—6s

1 day shirt
1 vest
1 underdrawers
1 pair socks
1 towel
2 handkerchiefs
1 wash rag
1 soap
1 toothbrush
1 tooth-powder

PARCEL D.—6s. (FOR INVALIDS

1lb. tin condensed milk
1lb. cocoa
½lb. sugar
1lb. Quaker oats
1lb. cod liver oil capsules
1 box extract of malt or ovo-
    maltine, or Mellin's Food
    (according to special require-
    ments)

A combined parcel of food and clothing, A and C or B and C, is dispatched for 10s., or special parcels can be sent.

For Bulgaria and Turkey there are three separate parcels, one of clothing, one of food for invalids, and another general parcel, containing food, tobacco or cigarettes.

The prisoners, in general, can themselves communicate with Berne and ask what they choose. I find that their chief requests are cheese, unsweetened tinned milk, butter, eggs, fruits, and vegetables, and, of course, tobacco.

Lady Grant Duff's gallant little organization has had all sorts of difficulties to face. There are shortages in neutral countries as well as in the countries at war. In Switzerland they lack string, cardboard, and many essentials, and the provision of these necessaries is quite an undertaking in itself.

I spent an interesting morning watching the preparation and testing of the bread, the opening of the mail from England containing the cheques and postal-orders and the 160 regimental lists, and finally the moving sight of the packing of the precious bread and its dispatch to our lonely war victims in Germany.

I could not help contrasting in my mind a visit I paid some time ago to a certain camp in England. Some of the Berne bread was going to Ruhleben, where our civilians have been for two years housed in a manner that has been graphically described by the American Embassy representatives.

The Germans in our hands are, in my personal opinion, treated with unnecessary and wasteful comfort. Their only deprivation is liberty. They are not at all grateful for their treatment. A German-Swiss gentleman who understands the Prussian character a great deal better than our powers-that-be told me that he knew that Prussia regards the indulgence of her prisoners in England as a sign of fear on the part of our Government, and that she considers that we are vainly trying to buy off Zeppelin raids and submarine piracy by ostentatious pampering of her people. A released English officer who had spoken to a German officer prisoner who had got home to Germany from Donington Hall stated that the German had the impertinence to try to persuade him that life in an officers' prison camp in Germany was exactly on a par with that at Donington Hall. He was absolutely ungrateful for the kindly treatment that he had received.

IV

GENEVA

PROPAGANDA TRICKS

MUCH valuable information can be gathered at Geneva in regard to the two important questions of prisoners and propaganda

Here are the headquarters of the old original Red Cross, founded in 1863. It would be impossible in anything less bulky than a fat quarto to deal with its innumerable energies. From Geneva radiate the communications on the subject of casualties, prisoners, their help, their finance, to every part of the theatres of war. The official title of the great Geneva organization is the " Comité International de la Croix Rouge." At the central office are some 300 assistants, voluntary and other, English, French, German, Austrian, Swiss, working under the same roof and labouring to do their best for the afflicted, their relatives and friends.

The extent of part of the work can be gauged from the fact that on certain days there are as many as 15,000 communications passing from one belligerent country to another through the office alone. Geneva is probably the chief centre of postal communication between Germany and England.

The important task of receiving and correcting the lists of prisoners is carried on here under a system that is as business-like as the management of a London bank. Some idea of the difficulties with which the

Lauzanne, editor of *Le Matin*, after a due period of military service, was sent to Switzerland, where he has done excellent work.

A distinguished French-Swiss explained the situation to me in the following words, which I noted at the time :—

The English should realize that Swiss military officers are, in the proportion of about three to one, pro-German, because they admire German military organization, because some of them have German kinsmen, have had German military training, or have married Germans. They recognize that Germany has perhaps under-estimated her task. The German Government, in order to create the impression in Switzerland that Germany is doing all the fighting, has made special arrangements, by a subvention, to distribute German newspapers and illustrated sheets specially throughout Switzerland. Look at this [he pointed to the *Illustrated Leipzig Gazette*] ; Switzerland is deluged with it week after week. It is beautifully printed in colours, the drawings are by the best German artists, the photographs are printed by a rotogravure. Here, you see, are English prisoners, almost unhurt, marching with their captors to the camp. Here, in another paper, you are being bombed out of your trenches by this or that gallant German regiment. We have had a little English propaganda here, but your people do not seem to study the methods of advertisers as the Germans do. German propaganda is ceaseless ; yours is feeble and intermittent. The German propaganda is in the hands of advertising people who understand that when an advertiser ceases to proclaim the virtue of his wares the sale of them disappears.

There are many weak points in the German

armour in Switzerland and other neutral countries, and they could be pierced by astute people who understand the psychology of each particular neutral nationality. Germany has always the advantage of propinquity in dealing with the Swiss, the Dutch, the Swedes, and the Danes. That is a fact that should not be forgotten by your propagandists, and should cause them to make exertions, greater, even, than the Germans themselves.

The force of this pro-Ally Swiss gentleman's remarks was borne in upon me when two or three days later I read in *Le Temps* a telegram to the following effect :—

The organization for German newspaper distribution at Zürich has presented to the large hotels at Geneva a form on which the owner or manager states that he is ready to place at the disposal of the public, in the reading-room of his hotel, the following newspapers and reviews :— *Der Tag*, of Berlin ; *Frankfurt Gazette, Cologne Gazette, Voss Gazette, Tägliche Rundschau*, of Berlin ; *Fremdenblatt*, of Hamburg ; *Leipzig Latest News, Illustrated Leipzig Gazette, Die Woche* (The Week), a Berlin illustrated paper ; *Reclams Universum*, Berlin illustrated journal; *Deutsche Politik* (German politics).

Under the terms of this agreement, it is pointed out that the German propagandists will deliver the newspapers and reviews free to the hotel, on condition that their display in the reading-room is not charged for.

The agreement is to take effect from September 1st to December 31st, 1916.

The *Journal de Génève* protests against this latest evolution of German propaganda.

Surely it would not be difficult for our Government to counteract this step by distributing supplies of the *Graphic* and *Illustrated London News*, with, if necessary, supplements in French and German, for circulation in Switzerland. The distribution would need to be watched by some shrewd man of business with Continental experience, who would counter the German news at every step.

I left Switzerland with two convictions, gathered from interviews with people who shall be nameless.

First, that the question of the treatment of our prisoners in Germany demands much greater attention that it is receiving.

Secondly, that if the British Government thinks that Swiss opinion is worth cultivating, in view of certain eventualities, it should take proper and prompt steps to combat German propaganda.

V

THE GERMANS IN SPAIN

The Army of Anti-Ally Workers

PAMPLONA, SPAIN

FORTY-SIX years ago Germany was at war with France over the question of the Spanish marriages and the Hohenzollern candidate, the initial cause of the Franco-Prussian conflict of 1870. Since that time the Germans have never ceased to agitate for the political and commercial control of Spain.

During the last two years, despite the war, they have managed by a stroke of good fortune, which at first sight looked like ill-luck, greatly to increase their numerical strength throughout the Peninsula.

In the last days of July, 1914, many Germans fled from France into Spain. Their number was speedily increased by the arrival at various Spanish ports of travelling Germans, who remained there, rather than face the Anglo-French blockade. When Portugal declared war there was another incursion of German refugees. To their number have since been added the German soldiers and civilians from Cameroon. It is said that altogether, including the large number of resident business Germans, there are now something like 80,000 Huns in Spain. The total is variously estimated at from 60,000 to 100,000, but a Barcelona man of affairs, who visits all parts of Spain continually, considers that, including the 20,000 residents of his own city, the number is approximately 80,000. That these 80,000 Germans are not idle is borne in upon one within a very few hours of crossing the Spanish frontier.

Let me first ask readers who have not recently visited Northern and Western Spain to remove from their thoughts all ideas gathered from Borrow or Ford. " Backward Spain," so far as the Northern provinces are concerned, is the land, not of gipsy, beggar, and brigand, but of Spanish, British, German enterprise, of highly-developed water-power, countless new light railways, automobiles, factories, workshops of all descriptions, and of hotels with bed-rooms and bath-rooms *en suite*.

Things are nowhere in the world as before the war. Thus, it is an unpleasant surprise, on going to a Spanish bank, to find that our good British sovereign, which, we were proud to think, was the standard coin of the world, is at an uncomplimentary discount in a land where one formerly received a handsome bonus in exchange. It is unpleasant, too, on opening countless Spanish newspapers, to find that a belief in German victory and in German invincibility is, apparently, a conviction in most parts of Spain. It is disappointing to be received by old Spanish friends, friends who have visited England, who know our country, with an air of doubt as to our capacity to make war. It is particularly disagreeable to notice the favourable and agreeable manner in which the Hun is received in Spanish society. And it is not flattering to the Allies to find that he has the support of a great body of the aristocracy, of practically the whole of the Church, Jesuit and otherwise, with, in addition, a large part of middle-class Spain.

I would not for a minute disregard the strong pro-Ally views of many Spaniards, some in important positions. We owe them a debt of gratitude. Many are labouring assiduously to convince their countrymen of the justice of our cause, but they are face to face with the hourly wireless propaganda from the Nauen station, Berlin, and the Austrian wireless from Pola. They have to encounter all manner of cross-currents beneath the sea of Spanish opinion, and these cross-currents have been forced by the Germans till in many cases they have become veritable tides of pro-Germanism.

It would be preposterous for a casual visitor to Spain, such as is the present writer, with but some half-dozen holiday tours in that country as a previous experience, to offer himself as an authority on a very complex subject. Yet he can, at least, record that which he hears from former Spanish acquaintances, from English and other residents, together with that which he reads, that which he sees.

I came here to Pamplona because it is a convenient German centre and because it is a pleasant place in a fair country. The days of early autumn in Northern Spain are crisp, yet warm, like the mimosa time in spring at Cannes. The Indian corn is now ripe; jasmine in great festoons and garlands, as we never see it in England, is everywhere, mixing its fragrance with that of the magnolia. The little, low-growing, purple wine-grapes in this, the famous Rioja district, are sweet enough to steal.

When one surveys these rich valleys, in which everything, including olives, bright red capsicums, vines, peaches, beets, tomatoes, all seem to luxuriate together in wild profusion, it is not difficult to understand why the men from the sandy plains of Prussia are covetous. There are other reasons of which I shall speak. A glance at the map of Europe should be sufficiently suggestive of Bismarck's anxieties about the Iberian Peninsula.

At the Café Kutz, at Pamplona, which, despite our blockade, bravely but falsely advertises Spaten-bräu-München on its wide white awning, may be found after *Mittagessen* many of the types of the German elements that are unceasingly working against us—and against Spain. One soon learns from their loud talk that the Germans in Spain have constituted themselves into a well-drilled army, obviously acting on definite instructions.

Just one typical scene. The Huns who were eating at one of the leading hotels to-day, and who had to bear our English-speaking as best they could, were probably mostly soldiers and civilians back from Cameroon. Their leader was a young Prussian of 30, whose neck and head were of about the same diameter. He had little, Oriental eyes, stiff wooden movements, a gash down the side of the face, received at a Mensur in student days, and hair cropped as closely as a poodle's.

Pamplona is a great clerical centre. A number of young priests were lunching, and heartily, let me say. As each left the room the young Boche rose and bent himself in half, in German fashion, with a tremendous bow, to the evident pleasure of the priests. The thing was exactly like the official railway courtesy ordered by telegram from Berlin to any more or less known foreign traveller, and at the same time showed the minute care with which the German army in Spain is working. With the Church on their side, the battle is half won. Later on, the same young Boche was one of a large company of noisy, hat-lifting Germans at the Kutz establishment, and it was amusing to notice that, as a flock of the black-robed fathers strolled by in an unmasculine costume (which is certainly not suited to Spanish heat and dust) the Huns cast amused and contemptuous glances behind their backs, and made slighting remarks about them.

From a Spanish acquaintance, who is not a little concerned at the growing intensity of German activity in Spain, I learned a good deal of the habits and customs of the propagandists, for such every one of them is.

Germany long ago impressed Spain with the prestige of her arms and her trade. On the Norte Railway the finest locomotives bear the name of their German place of origin, in legible letters, that can be read by passengers on both of the station platforms. At one time Spanish locomotives came from England. In the home, or the hotel, there is nearly always a German piano, a German bath, and you switch on a German electric lamp to see the time by a German clock. The chemists' shops are full of German drugs and preparations.

A vast, new, many-windowed, oblong, ugly, industrial building looms up before you at the corner of a road, and you find that it is a sugar factory erected by Germans, *since* the war.

The average Spaniard, who is more of a *caballero* than a man of business, is naturally impressed by years of German commercial surroundings. Many Spanish business men are frankly afraid of Germans.

The khaki-clad officers and men of the Spanish Army—especially the younger officers—looking uncommonly like our Belgian Allies except for the shape of their caps, are, I was assured by Spanish officers, convinced that Germany must win.

From the moment of the outbreak of war every refugee as he arrived was immediately set to work to learn Spanish. Many of them had fled into Spain so hurriedly that they were without funds, and these were provided by the local German Consuls. But the invaders were not long idle. The majority obtained work in the innumerable establishments of their compatriots, some in Barcelona, some at Seville, some in the iron districts, others in the countless industries in Spain into which the German vampire has dug its claws. A few, it is believed, have availed themselves of their knowledge of Spanish to escape, as Spaniards, to South America, to Holland, and to Scandinavia. For the purpose of such adventurous journeys they buy up old passports, or make use of others, manufactured for the special purpose.

But, as a rule, the Germans in Spain show no great anxiety to get back to the land of the meatless day and the bread-ticket. They look prosperous and well-fed, and they are unquestionably helping to get Spain into the German clutch. They realize that if to a victorious Germany Spain is very useful, to a defeated Germany Spain is almost essential.

In the likely event of the development of overland transport by aeroplane, the coasts and harbours of friendly Spain would be invaluable to Germany. The mineral wealth of the Peninsula, only now being scientifically developed, would afford her several sorts of raw material, of which Germany has little or none. And, as an outlet for German goods, as the main point of departure for the wealthy Republics of South America, as a bulwark against English control of Gibraltar, Spain is, from the German point of view, distinctly Germany's " pidgin."

The well-drilled battalions of German residents and refugees in Spain know exactly how to confuse public opinion in any locality. In the North of Spain, where the French have never been popular since the Napoleonic invasion, they alarm the ignorant by threats that an Allied victory might mean a revival of the days of a hundred years ago. In the West they state that, as a reward for Portugal's " treachery " in joining the Allies, she is to be given two of the richest Spanish provinces.

Lately Spain became anxious on this point, coupled as it was with the statement that the Portuguese Army was mobilized against Spain. The Portuguese Government wisely asked Spain to send a military mission to inspect the situation. There was not, of course, a word of truth in the statement, which was industriously promulgated by one of the most widely circulated Madrid newspapers, the *A.B.C.*, which,

under a cunning pretence of neutrality, is, as I can
easily prove by its files, subtly and continually pro-
German. The Portuguese Government has had the
wisdom to cut off the Portuguese circulation of the
A.B.C. One illustration from the *A.B.C.* will suffice.
It may be found on page 8 of the first edition of September 3 at the beginning of an article headed " The
Military Situation." I translate it roughly and ap-
pend the original Spanish :—

"The *great* Franco-English offensive may be
regarded as broken. The results obtained, after
two months' fighting, are practically *nil*, and it
must be admitted, besides, that most of the
little that has been won is due to the effort of
the French troops ; whereby it is demonstrated
that armies cannot be improvised.

"The operations on the Somme have hardly
influenced the position at Verdun ; since, if
it is certain that for some time past the Germans
have not been attacking, they retain the positions
conquered, and the repeated efforts of the French
against Thiaumont and Fleury have not changed
the situation. To all appearances, it does not
seem that, for the present, events of importance
are in preparation on the Western front.

"On the Isonzo, the Italians remain unable
to go beyond Gorizia ; if it costs them as much
to get out as it did to get in, they will have to
wait still many a month."

[La *gran* ofensiva franco-inglesa en el Somme
puede darse por fracasada : los resultados ob-
tenidos, después de dos meses de combates, son
prácticamente nulos, y cabe augurar, además,
que lo poco que se ha conseguido se debe en su
mayor parte al esfuerzo de las tropas francesas ;
con lo cual queda demostrado que los Ejércitos
no se improvisan.

Las operaciones en el Somme apenas han influido en el campo de Verdun, pues si bien es cierto que hace tiempo que los alemanes no atacan, conservan las posiciones conquistadas, y las repetidas tentativas de los franceses contra Thiaumont y Fleury no han modificado la situación. Verosímilmente, no parece que se preparan, por ahora, en el teatro occidental, acontecimientos de importancia.

En el Isonzo, los italianos siguen sin poder salir de Goricia ; si les cuesta tanto la salida como la entrada, hay que esperar aún muchos meses.]

The article proceeds to deal in the same style with the Russian and Rumanian operations, and concludes by comparing the position of Greece with that of Spain in 1808.

Not content with this essay in perversion, the *A.B.C.* had the impudence to publish on page 20 of the same issue an editorial note entitled " Our Neutrality," calling upon its readers to bear witness to its entire impartiality whenever they hear it called in question !

In the south " Gibraltar for the Spaniards " remains the most successful German cry, appealing as it does to Spanish pride and sentiment. The Moroccan question and the Moroccans themselves are never let alone by Germany. The suggestion is continually put forward, too, that Germany stands for monarchy, order, and religion ; whereas England is the home of free speech and industrial unrest, and France the centre of anarchy.

Next to our own island, Spain is the chief mother country of the world. Here and there the Spaniards exhibit maps showing to what parts of the earth Spanish stock has carried the Spanish language. With the language has gone a certain amount of

sympathy for Spain. The Germans know that, with
Spain as a *point d'appui*, and the backing of Spanish
opinion, and, above all, with that of the Church,
their cause is likely to be better appreciated in the
New World than if mother-Spain were hostile. From
Spain, therefore, proceeds to South America a great
deal of German propaganda in the Spanish language.

Although many war fortunes are being made in
Spain—for she is supplying iron to England, railway
trucks and war material of other descriptions to
France—some discomfort has been caused by the
war. One of the most unpopular topics in Spain
is the high price of bread. Another is the cost
of coal, which in some places stands at £6 a ton.
These circumstances are used by the German agents
to stir up feeling against England for her wickedness
in launching the world into war.

The chief methods of propaganda, then, seem
to be a daily stream of wireless *communiqués* from
Berlin and Austria, discrediting the Allies ; continuous
activity on the part of the Church and the Carlists ;
the influence of the German " colony," with steady
work on the part of the university professors and
schoolmasters on behalf of the Central Powers, the
chief channel being, of course, the Press. There
are notable exceptions, such as the *Imparcial, El
Liberal, Heraldo,* and others engaged in sustained
effort to put the truth about the war before the
Spanish public. These efforts have, especially of
late, had a considerable amount of success, and have
aroused German hostility, as will no doubt this and
another article of mine. A small, but, it is to be
hoped, a growing part of Spanish opinion is disgusted
with German cruelties, and more especially with
the wholesome enslavement of Belgian and French
women in the invaded provinces. There has been
talk in the English newspapers of a remonstrance
by the Spanish Government in this matter, but

in the absence of much stronger pro-Ally propaganda and much firmer British diplomacy, it would be surprising were anything really important to result.[1]

Let me give a few instances as showing the methods of presenting news to the Spanish public by certain journals. In all the neutral countries German Press agents represent England as cowering under the Zeppelin terror. To-day, in one newspaper, I read of a great Zeppelin raid on London, and of orders by the Metropolitan Police that not a single ray of light was to be emitted at night, either out of doors or indoors. This news was prominently given— but not a word was said in this journal about one of the raiding Zeppelins having been destroyed.

In one of our headquarters' *communiqués* the other day it was stated that we brought down a certain number of enemy aeroplanes. The *communiqué* was so put as to give the impression that *we* had lost the aeroplanes, and the heading was, " The British Communiqué. Ten Aeroplanes Lost."

This sort of thing, carried on day after day and week after week by innumerable journals among a people who have had German efficiency drilled into them for years, is a sort of poison that will only be removed by some great military success on our part. Verdun has done as much as anything to cure a certain part of Spanish public opinion of the " German invincibility " theory. (It is interesting, by the way, to note here, in Pamplona, a German centre, little books for sale, with the head of the Kaiser so drawn as to look like a skull on a background of blood, entitled simply " Verdun.") Former Spanish acquaintances of pro-German views admitted to me that Verdun was puzzling to them.

As elsewhere, the view is industriously spread by Germany that England is the sole and only

[1] Up to the time of going to press, as we say in Fleet-street, no remonstrance has been made.

cause of the war, and that the unfortunate French are only too anxious to make peace. England, the might of whose army is absolutely unknown to the average Spaniard, is represented as sacrificing France, as she is alleged to have sacrificed Belgium, Serbia, Montenegro. If, runs the argument, Spain were so mad as to join the Allies, her fate would be that of France and the rest ; and if she were even to exhibit friendly neutrality civil war would result. The leading Carlist papers have recently headed their articles " Neutrality or Civil War ! "

President Wilson, who, like most Americans, is not liked in Spain, by reason of the loss of Cuba, and whose Mexican policy is not pleasing to a country that has millions invested in that distraught El Dorado, is quite a hero of the Germanophiles. When the pro-Ally Spaniards ask the pro-Germans when they are going to protest against German horrors, the pro-German reply is that the atrocities are malicious inventions of John Bull. If they were true, the good President Wilson would interfere in the matter.

Another line taken by German propagandists, chiefly among the aristocratic classes, is that Spain should keep herself strictly impartial, so that, if necessary, King Alfonso and his Cabinet may perhaps be invited by Great Britain to arbitrate when we sue for peace with Germany. That we shall eventually invite the Spanish Court to save our face seems to be accepted by all except the inner circle, who know some of the facts.

One of these facts is that the Germans lately induced a well-known Spanish nobleman to go to London to fly a peace kite, and that, on his arrival, those to whom he was accredited wisely took not the least notice of him. The Germans now assert that the unfortunate Spaniard went to London on his own account.

s

From much that I have heard in the course of my enquiries, the Spanish Court would be the very worst arbiter between the Allies and the Central Powers. Whatever may be King Alfonso's own knowledge, the views of the average Court official are something like these :—

" English officers are gallant fellows, excellent polo players, good sportsmen in general, but amateurs. The English ' Tommies ' are few in number, brave, but foolhardy. The ' bloody repulses ' so often mentioned in the German *communiqués* are due to the fact that an army cannot be raised in a few years. France has called up all her men from 17 years of age to 48. England can do nothing on land of any service. Therefore Germany is bound to win, and even if she does not win, cannot possibly lose."

I am informed that a Spanish military mission has been sent to British military headquarters. It is to be trusted that it will have come back with opinions that may somewhat change this Court point of view, though I am doubtful of the lasting effect of anything short of a smashing and palpable military defeat of Germany—one that cannot be disproved by wireless.

Former Spanish acquaintances regard me as something of a hero in venturing across the German submarine-controlled Channel at this juncture. Others doubt that I really propose to go back to live and work in Zeppelin-infested London. One hears all sorts of stupid nonsense, from people who ought to know better, such as the statement that Princess Henry of Battenberg, mother of the Queen of Spain, has come to Spain for safety from Zeppelins. These views would be merely annoying were it not that they have a bearing on Spanish opinion during the war and on the theory of German invincibility.

A good deal of travel among neutrals lately has borne in upon me the fact that no one wants to be on the losing side. It is obviously with this view in mind that Germany keeps her 80,000 agents in Spain perpetually at work, hiding Allied successes, minimizing the importance of such events as the intervention of Rumania—which shook a small section of Spanish opinion for a day or two—and belittling the British effort. A shrewd Englishman of business in Spain—and we have many such—assured me that he believed the present melancholy state of our good English pound sterling was due not only to the balance of trade against us but to the doubt as to our capacity to stand up against Germany. Former Spanish admirers who have been impressed by the German propaganda are politely silent when some idea is given them of the determination of Great Britain and her Allies to crush the vampire.

Pro-Ally Spaniards say that immeasurable harm was done in the long months during which the British Army issued no daily *communiqué* whatever. The impression was then almost indelibly confirmed that we had no Army. Yet during all that time we had taken our part in the battles of the Marne, the Aisne, and Ypres.

There are quick minds at the other end of the German wireless and they watch our proceedings very closely. They flood Spain with downright lies, minimizing statements and contradictions with a celerity which is quite amazing. I have been so struck again and again by the quickness with which neutrals learn from Germany what is going on, that I recently asked Commendatore Marconi if it were possible that the Germans had a secret wireless in our midst. He replied that it would be quite possible for them to have wireless apparatus, that it would be very difficult to detect, and that he himself would be able to erect a wireless in England that our authorities would have great trouble in discovering. But it is certain that what we are,

s 2

in reality, face to face with, is great alertness
and intelligence on the part of the German Press
Bureau.

The Germans in Spain have wealthy people among
them who have seen to it that the various German
communities and individuals are closely linked up.
The newcomers are gathering every sort of information
about Spanish industries and the possibilities of
development in Spain. Need I point out that, with
a population of less than twenty millions, 80,000
active propagandists and workers constitute a formidable body ?

The number may be 80,000, it may be slightly
more or less, but the Hun seems to be everywhere.
Almost the first words I heard in Spain were German.
Seven out of ten of the numerous provincial journals
are, more or less, Germanophile.

In a motor journey of some 1,300 kilometres
I encountered German pedestrian and motor parties
all bound on the same purposeful work. Their
task is the easier because the general Spanish public
is not vastly interested in the war. In Spain it
is not the vital question that it is in England, in
France, or even Switzerland. In the newspapers
our Great Crusade often takes quite a minor position,
and in the majority there is more about the bull
fight or the latest crime than about the greatest
event in the world's history.

VI

A SPANISH TOUR

SOME PEOPLE AND PLACES

WHILE it is difficult for anyone who has seen anything of the horrors of the German invasion of Belgium and France to comprehend the neutral frame of mind, it has to be remembered in visiting and contrasting Spain, where there is no sign of conflict, that her people are at peace.

A few of the more far-seeing Spanish leaders do not quite like that situation. There is a good deal of jealousy of little Portugal, who has not been afraid to throw down her glove to the Kaiser. But, on the whole, Spain in general, and industrial Spain in particular, appears to be glad to be out of the maelstrom.

In the course of visits extending over 30 years I have never known such prosperity in Spain as at present. With the exception of a few old women who haunt the doors of cathedrals and a single gipsy, who, by the way, asked alms in very fair German—imagining, I regret to say, that our party was from the Fatherland—we were not assailed by a single beggar anywhere. Good fortune seems to smile everywhere alike, in town and country. San Sebastian and other watering-places are having seasons such as they have never known before. In more than one of the excellent motorists' hotels erected during the past few years we found it difficult to obtain sleeping quarters.

On setting out on a visit to the iron districts, we made the journey by the wonderful coast road *via* Zarauz, Bilbao, and Santander, certainly the most majestic, if dangerous, cliff road I have travelled in a somewhat extensive experience. The Bay of Naples, the road from Larne to Portrush, or the Grande Corniche cannot compare with it. The only drawbacks are the dust and nerve-racking corners, round which tear high-powered cars, with open exhausts, at a speed that reminds one of the Continental road races of a decade back.

There is a noise like that of a Zeppelin, or a traction engine. Our modest 20 h.p. car is passed as if standing still, and then dust, that completely obscures the view of sea and sky.

" The King ! " cries our chauffeur. His amiable Majesty is *en route*. Youth will be served. Further on we find a powerful Royal car—not, fortunately, Alfonso's—in a ditch, with the two front wheels off. A day or two afterwards the Spanish papers record yet another and serious accident to certain members of the Royal entourage.

In numberless ways it is a strange sensation to be living in surroundings not unlike those of the Riviera years ago in peace time. The white wings of the racing yachts are in the bay, golfing and lawn tennis parties are setting out for the day's sport, immaculately-dressed young Spaniards, with Bond Street and Savile Row written all over their clothes, are escorting Señoritas, dressed from the Rue de la Paix. The whole thing, against the background of the war, is like a dream of something long past.

The road continues, one long film of beautiful pictures, though it passes through the iron districts leading to Bilbao and beyond. There is nothing in the nature of a black country, or manufacturing Lancashire, or chemical Cheshire. Now and then one is on the Riviera, in a few moments in the sad mountains of Donegal. The hot southern sun blazes down on little inland coves of the Atlantic, in which are ensconced tiny watering-places; but there are no wounded, as in France or at home. Villas, embowered in walnut and chestnut trees, with gardens gay with red and white roses, and the universal jasmine and pink oleander, have carefully closed *persiennes* to keep out the mid-day heat.

As one approaches Bilbao the hills are red with the iron-laden soil from beneath which is brought down by vertical railway and wireways the metal for the guns and the shells. The rivers and their estuaries pour, brilliant red, into the green Atlantic. One of our party remarked that, if anyone painted this contrast of sea and river, he would be regarded as an unusually eccentric Futurist. It was pleasantly cool sauntering along, but when we stopped for luncheon at Bilbao, the centre of one of the richest mineral territories in the world, we found that the day was as hot as midsummer at home.

In the restaurant our next neighbour is a stout German lady, whose performance on the tooth-pick would have done credit to a restaurant in the Friedrichstrasse in Berlin. We English speakers receive the usual glares from the Germans, who are sharing the excellent meal provided.

Afterwards, a Spaniard to whom we have an introduction, complains of the Allies' commercial black-list. We point out that war is war, and that the saving of Allied lives and the destruction of enemy trade is more important to us than commercial relations with neutrals. His reply is that the rule should be applied all round, and especially to certain iron mines which are conjointly owned by Germans and English, and he mentions Krupp and an English firm by name. He admits that the district is largely Germanophile, and he believes that considerable iron is going into Germany by Norway. This statement

is afterwards denied, although not absolutely, by
an English authority whom we consulted.

After sauntering through an incredibly beautiful
country, with delicious glimpses of the Atlantic,
passing rivers in which the trout were rising tempt-
ingly, and one in which there was excellent salmon
fishing, we slept at Oviedo, at a palatial hotel as unlike
the Spain of 20 years ago as could be imagined. At
the local garage there was an assemblage of motor-
cars of the first rank, and not one of them, we
are glad to say, was German. Rolls-Royce,
Renault, Delaunay-Belleville, a Daimler, and the
Hispano-Suiza predominated.

There is an old Oviedo and a new which is being
built as rapidly and noisily as new New York, and as
ugly as new Buenos Aires.

Wakened in the morning by the sound of blasting
in the neighbouring hills, a sound that is never out
of one's ears in industrialized Spain, we crawled up
the zigzags of the great Cordilleras Cantabricas, and
suddenly descended from the dense, wet clouds into
what was exactly like Egypt. Red and ochre hills,
a great blazing, yellow plain, dried-up looking towns
on the hillside, pigeon cotes exactly like those in
Egyptian villages, and water raised by shadoofs.
The wheat has been gathered, and in some places is
being trodden out, as in Biblical times. In all places
it is winnowed in the wind, in ancient fashion.

Out on the plain the only birds are hawks and
quail-like partridges, with also our own red-legs.
We stopped the car outside an adobe hut of Moorish
design, thick-walled and very cool within. The
bright-eyed, dark, dry-skinned peasant, who comes out
to tell us the way, invites us to taste some of the wine
grapes which, together with some quinces, he is
growing in his little oasis. He is extremely intelligent,
declines any payment, as is usual in rural Spain, but

accepts a cigar and a few picture papers—for he
cannot read—and asks us about the war. It has
had the effect of raising the price of bread. The
land as far as we can see, he tells us, belongs to a
great nobleman, and is worked on a feudal system.
Owing to the emigration to South America, labour is
scarce, and he and his work doubly hard in consequence,
It would be good land, he says, if the rain were
attracted by the planting of more trees. The war,
he fears, will be long. His good manners, which
previous experience has taught me to find everywhere
and among all classes in Spain, forbid him expressing
an opinion as to the result.

Later on that day a similar enquiry as to our route
from an old labourer brought the question : Were
we French ? " No," we replied, " English." He
put out his hand and shook ours warmly, saying that
he had been in the service of an English family in
Buenos Aires. And the war ? How long will it
last ? Long, he feared. " The Allemans are
strong."

There is no country in which I have been where
one is asked so frequently : How long will the war
last ? The war seems to be some great distant
monster which, despite the people's interest in their
own everyday life, is ever, if distantly, present.

The dust between Albert and Arras, in the earlier
days of the battle of the Somme, when thousands of
troops, transport wagons, and mules were stirring it,
seemed to be, to use an Americanism, the " extension
of the limit." Egyptian dust is perpetual and in-
sinuating, and Indian dust is like khaki flour. But
Spanish dust, in August, when a Norther is blowing,
amounts to something like a perpetual fog. A closed
car is of no avail; goggles worn within it are useless.
A passing mule can raise a cloud of it, and it was
consoling to think, whatever may be the difficulties

in front of our soldiers in that part of the map in which Sir Douglas Haig and General Foch are operating, a war in this part of the world would be worse, a veritable agony of thirst.

Yet, little more than a hundred years ago, the great Duke's soldiers drove Soult's forces across waterless plains similar to these, at a time when there were none of the comforts of mechanical transport.

The contrast between the peace and gaiety of small Spanish towns at night, and our thoughts of France at this time is trying.   Yet no one who has been in a neutral country would wish to live in its atmosphere rather than in that of England or of her Allies.   These Spanish towns are alive with children, who, having like all Spaniards, enjoyed their *siesta*, appear to go to bed about the time people are pouring out of the theatres in London.

Almost every small centre has an excellent band, whose only fault is the monotony of its mournful, modern Spanish music, which seems to be almost always written in the minor.   It is that of a people resigned to their lost position as *conquistadores*.

Often, it is pleasant to note, we came across places in which there were not only no Germans, but no knowledge of Germans.   In some districts where there were Germans the people were perfectly frank in their dislike of them.   The Spaniards are extremely good mimics, and can imitate German ways in a most amusing manner.

Enquiries and researches in a good many quarters, every one of which revealed the same steady German purpose, brought us eventually back to San Sebastian, which many of its admirers claim, perhaps with reason, to be the most beautiful seaside resort in the world.   San Sebastian to-day is humming with life and visitors.   On the way into the town we meet a small English jockey, heavily swathed, toiling at

least four miles an hour in the afternoon sun, to
reduce his weight for the racing, which takes place
almost daily. The local bull ring is packed, and an
attempt to get a seat for a pelota match was in
vain.

Although the Spaniards are still the proud people
they have always been, there is that curious mixture
of democracy that makes San Sebastian a combination of Monte Carlo and Margate. The King and his
yacht are here. Most of the Embassies have moved
here from Madrid. All Spain that counts fills the
beautiful villas on the hills, and the densely packed
hotels. In the morning the perfect sands swarm
with children.

Along the promenade that leads to Miramar,
outside which lounge his Majesty's guards in pic-
turesque red Biscayan caps, there is an endless procession of tramcars and motors, mingled with slowly
moving, yoked oxen, and the perpetual donkey of the
peasants, as often as not ridden pillion. The casino
is, of course, the main attraction of this very rapidly
growing town. In the gaming rooms, as at Monte
Carlo, are the same shabby old ladies, with solemn
faces, deliberately placing their five pesetas, with the
other and younger ladies, who throw their money
away as rapidly as they get it. Here and there is
an Englishman, who looks thoroughly ashamed at
being caught gambling in war-time, with the customary wizened old men, studiously working out
their systems. There are Germans here, as everywhere, but they chiefly have their headquarters at
their own *café* in the town. A German in Spain is
not, as a rule, on pleasure bent.

A pleasing and quite harmless feature of the
casino at San Sebastian is the organized gathering
of hundreds of children on the great terrace outside,
and in the rooms not devoted to gambling. The
absence of black in the women's and children's dresses

is a striking contrast to one who has just come from France, and, were it not for an occasional mantilla, there would be nothing but the vivid greens, yellows, and blues that sound so bizarre, but are not out of place in Spain, where the national colours of red and yellow fit the landscape as properly as do the green, white, and red of sunlit Italy. The Spaniards make much of their children. Sometimes one feels that the small people are a little out of place at the hotel dinner hour, which is usually at 8.30 or 9 o'clock. As a rule the children are beautifully dressed, well cared for, most attractive, and altogether *sans gênes*. When we asked a Spanish friend why that vivacious and quick-witted creature, the *chico* (the Spanish boy) develops so quickly into something like apathetic languor, he replied it was " the education." Certainly the contrast between the early manhood of Spain and the alertness of the boys is very remarkable.

San Sebastian is itself solemnly and particularly interesting to English people, who have a pilgrimage of their own near by.

And so, leaving the Casino, with its myriads of little ones, who were being entertained by the sending up of grotesque fire balloons, in the shape of all manner of animals and black men, and escaping from the noise of the two rival bands, we said good-bye to neutral Spain, by visiting the scene of the famous and gloriously victorious storming of the citadel in 1813, when our soldiers showed exactly the same qualities they are displaying on the Somme to-day. They crossed the river under a terrible fire, which filled it with English blood. They performed what seemed the impossible, and what was almost as remarkable as Wolfe's attack on Quebec.

At the summit of the citadel are a few English graves, which seem somewhat more neglected than they should be. From this lofty scene of the great

struggle they look straight out towards the Bay of
Biscay to England. The most legible inscription
is as follows :—

*Sacred to the memory of Lieutenant-Colonel
Sir Richard Fletcher, Bart. ; Captain C. Rhodes,
Captain G. Collyer, Lieutenant H. Machell, Corps
of Royal Engineers, who fell at the siege of San
Sebastian, August 31, 1813.*

INDEX

279

T

INDEX

PRINTED IN GREAT BRITAIN BY R. CLAY AND SONS, LTD.,
BRUNSWICK STREET STAMFORD STREET, S.E., AND BUNGAY, SUFFOLK.